The Oldest Old in Everyday Life

Self Perception, Coping With Change, and Stress

Ruth Dunkle, PhD, Beverly Roberts, RN,
and Marie Haug, PhD

Springer Publishing Company

0024342

Ruth E. Dunkle, MSW, direct service/aging, 1973, Syracuse University; Ph.D., Social Science, 1978, Syracuse University. Professor Dunkle's research, teaching and clinical practice focus on gerontology. Recent research projects include "The Use of Social Services Among Families of Dementia Patients" (with Sara Leitsch) funded by the Michigan Alzheimer's Disease Research Center and "An Historical Examination of the Delivery of Social Services by a Private Foundation in Detroit Michigan, 1929–1971 (with Timothy Wintermute and Amy Schiller) funded by the Hannan Foundation. Since 1988, Professor Dunkle has served as a project co-director of the National Institute of Aging's training program, "Social Research Training on Applied Issues of Aging." She also serves as co-director of the Hartford Foundation Implementation Grant, "Strengthening Geriatric Social Work."

Beverly L. Roberts, PhD, FAAN, FGSA, is Professor and Associate Dean of Academic Programs at the Frances Payne Bolton School of Nursing of Case Western Reserve University. She is also a Senior Faculty Associate of the University Center of Aging and Health at the university. Dr. Roberts has devoted her more than twenty-year research career on exercise and physical and psychosocial factors that affect physical and psychological capacities required for performance of daily activities. Dr. Roberts has presented and published widely on these topics and has participated in program grants that prepare health care professionals to care for elderly adults.

Marie R. Haug, PhD, received her doctorate in sociology from Case Western Reserve University where she taught from 1968 until 1999. In addition to being Professor Emerita of Sociology, she is also Director Emerita of the University's Center of Aging and Health. She has published widely in books and professional journals such as the *Journal of Gerontology*, the *Journal of Health and Social Behavior*, and *Medical Care*. Dr. Haug co-edited *Elderly Patients and Their Doctors; Depression and Aging: Causes, Care, and Consequences; Communications Technology and the Elderly: Issues and Forecasts; Arthritis and the Elderly;* and *The Physical and Mental Health of Aged Women*. She has also co-authored *Consumerism in Medicine: Challenging Physician Authority*.

THe Oldest Old
in Everyday Life

Self Perception, Coping With Change, and Stress

Springer Publishing Company, Inc.
536 Broadway
New York, NY 10012-3955

Acquisitions Editor: Helvi Gold
Production Editor: Janice G. Stangel
Cover design by Susan Hauley

01 02 03 04 05 / 5 4 3 2 1

Library of Congress Cataloging-in-Publication Data

The oldest old in everyday life : self perception, coping with change, and stress / Ruth Dunkle, Beverly Roberts, and Marie Haug, authors.
    p. cm.
  Includes bibliographical references and index.
  ISBN 0-8261-1385-0
  1. Aged—Longitudinal studies. 2. Aging—Psychological aspects—Longitudinal studies. 3. Aged—Health and hygiene—Longitudinal studies. I. Dunkle, Ruth E. II. Roberts, Beverly L. III. Haug, Marie R.
  HQ1061 .O42 2001
  305.26—dc21

                                                                 00-064095
                                                                    CIP

Printed in Canada by Tri-Graphic Printing

To Earl and Karl, the best gifts I ever got.

RED

To Drew Roberts, whose support & encouragement were instrumental in many of my accomplishments. To my grandmother, Grace Huntsman who was engaged in life and the world around her.

BLR

To Fred Haug, who was active up to his nineties.

MRH

Contents

0024342

Preface

There is something fascinating about people who have outlived their projected lifetime, people who are "statistically dead." The people about whom this book is written were born near the turn of the 20th century, when life expectancy was 47 years. Few anticipated living to an age that would nearly double this expectancy. In most instances, they lived longer than their spouses and, more remarkably, their own children.

As a social work practitioner at a geriatric clinic at the University of Michigan Hospitals, I saw many patients in this age group. What was surprising was the variability in coping strategies within a group of elders who had lost many things: their health, loved ones, homes, and so on. Many found joy in living day to day; others spent much of their time complaining about all that was no longer possible. Availability of resources—physical, financial, and social—did not seem to explain these differences. Often, those with resources found little joy in life. In many cases, the people who found little joy in life had more resources than those who enjoyed their lives had. What were their lives like? How did they cope with the changes they faced? No information was available for exploring these questions.

In an effort to learn more about very old people, we responded to a request for proposal (RFP) form the National Institute on Aging (NIA) in 1985 to study these very old people, those over the age of 85. Very little if anything was known about people in this age group. Census data were only gathered on those 75 year of age or older, blending the old-old, as they have been called, with the very old. The increasing number of people in the very old category drew attention to these people, but nothing was known about their lives. The issuing of the RFP drew researcher attention to this need.

We were funded in 1986 to conduct a longitudinal study that would allow us to follow nearly 200 people over the age of 85 during an 18-month period. This project was entitled *The Effect of Stress on the Physical Functioning of Those over the Age of 85 Years.* We would have liked to have had a younger comparison group or even a longitudinal study in which we could follow participants from earlier points in their lives into very old age, but this was not financially feasible. We settled for a convenience sample of community dwellers over the age of 85.

No study had addressed the relationship between functional capacity and stressors and worry among persons aged 85 and over. Furthermore, the variability of functional levels in relation to mortality was little understood. Existing knowledge of the very old was limited and largely negative, such as statistics on various chronic diseases and mortality, or largely speculative, such as the views about the impact of losses or stressful life events. How these oldest old people coped with what they experienced, what factors promoted functional ability, and what relationship exists between such functional ability and postponement of mortality remained open for investigation. An evaluation of the coping strategies and impact of mediating factors on functional capacity was necessary to ensure an understanding of the dynamic relationship between stress and function. By determining the circumstances under which the elder was able to cope with the loss and change often associated with being very old and potentially to minimize the effects of these stressors on function, the complex nature of the process could be understood and the elder's health and well-being promoted. Our research was designed to close gaps in knowledge by studying these issues among old-old people who remained noninstitutionalized. The use of a longitudinal design added another new dimension, that of assessing the process of stress and coping over time among this most vulnerable but surviving age group.

Until this point, the research on stress had only made a clear connection between stress and health in older people, not functional ability. As their stress increased, their health deteriorated. With our belief that these very old people were more fragile than younger older people, we hypothesized that we would find a significant relationship between stress and worry and functional abilities.

We found that stress, discrete events in their lives such as the deaths of loved ones or change in residence, and so on, were much less of an issue for these elders than was the worry that came with everyday life. The older respondents worried about such things as the health of their friends and family, having to change residence in the future as their own health deteriorated, and needing more help. Worry was a more significant predictor of decline in activities of daily living than was stress.

When we designed this study, we thought that 18 months, although not a very long period of time, would be long enough to produce significant change in health and function among these very old people. We were wrong. Although these people did change in these main areas, it was not in significant ways. All of the people in the sample at Wave 1 lived in the community but not in retirement communities or nursing homes, where they would have had formal help available to them. We purposefully started the study with a more independently functioning group, but we misjudged the slowness of their decline. At the end of the 18-month (four data gathering points) study, there was little change in our dependent variables, physical activities of daily living, and instrumental activities of daily living. In 1995 we were funded for a fifth wave of data collection by the University of Michigan's Office of the Vice President for Research. We wanted to see what had happened in the lives of these very old people during the 7 years since the end of the NIA project. In particular, we wanted to examine the relationship between stress and function with greater variability in function than was the case through the first four waves.

In writing this book, we hope to appeal to a wide audience of researchers, students, and practitioners in the health and psychosocial arenas. Specifically, practitioners in nursing, social work, and psychology as well as academic gerontologists may be interested in reading this book. By focusing the chapters on well-researched topics, such as self-perception, coping, functioning and mortality, and goals for the future, we were able to extend existing knowledge to those over the age of 85.

Overall the study was illuminating. These older people were engaged in life and maintained contact with people who were able to provide support throughout the study. In these ways they did not differ from older people who were younger than our participants. We were surprised, however, to find differences between those participants in their 80s and those in their 90s.

Initially, we looked at all those in the sample above age 85, the overall group labeled oldest-old. As we progressed with the analyses, it became apparent that those in their 90s were different from how they had been when they were in their 80s. For instance, many participants worried about their decline in health and functional abilities in their 80s but did not have these same worries when they arrived in their 90s. It was not because their health was any better; in most instances it was not. These elders saw themselves as fortunate for just being alive.

Bernice Neugarten, a renowned gerontologist, initially described the distinction between the young old and old-old (75+) but mentioned the changing landscape of older people and the continued extension of life. This prescient view helped us move beyond the "old-old" group to the "oldest-old." No doubt there will be future gerontologists studying a new group of "oldest-old" for the new millennium.

We hope that this book will help those of you who care for and are interested in very old people provide better care and, more importantly, discover their uniqueness in not only what they need but also what they have to offer.

CHAPTER 1

The Old Growing Older: An Overview

This book describes the experiences, aspirations, and attitudes of a group of people in their 80s and 90s who live in a Midwestern urban area. This group includes the 23 still-active survivors of a sample of 193 such aged subjects whose diminishing numbers were followed in 5 data collection waves over 9 years between 1986 and 1995. Details of the interview procedures and methods of sampling are given in chapter 2, laying the basis for the following findings.

Five subsequent chapters address these findings, which cover aspects of the beliefs and experiences of these very old and rarely studied octogenarians and nongenerations. Thus, in chapter 3 their self-perceptions are explored in a unique set of materials concerning those over the age of 85. Chapter 4 covers still another entirely new issue in aging research: the views and plans of the very old about the future. Particular attention is paid to the relationship of goals to the mental health of elders who are very old.

Chapter 5 covers another topic not previously addressed with respect to those more than 80 years old: how they cope with their everyday problems. With some avenues closed because of the person's age and with many special difficulties arising for the same reason, this is a particularly relevant chapter. Chapter 6 focuses on related problems significant to the very old, their declining healthful functioning, and the certainty of their future demise. Finally, chapter 7 outlines services and resources that could meet the needs of this unique, growing group of the oldest old.

These characteristics occur in the context of national patterns of the aging process. As has often been documented, the fastest growing segment in the U.S. population consists of those 65 and older. Less well-known is that the segment age 85 and over is growing faster still, and there is even a disproportionate growth spurt among centenarians (Grundy, 1997; Perls & Silver, 1999) projected to reach 100,000 by the year 2000 (Larkin, 1999). These demographic developments, even if at present only offering estimates for the future, nevertheless argue for exploration of the problems and potentials of current aged cohorts as they grow older. Most published U.S. Census data are useless for securing information on the oldest-old. Reports are usually given only for the category age 65+ and rarely for those 75 and over (Bureau of the Census, 1997). In order to identify characteristics of those at least in the 85 and over cohort, it is necessary to consult special studies with access to unpublished census tapes or to research subgroups in their 80s, 90s, or 100s.

THE AGED POPULATION

One of the most comprehensive reviews of what data are available is found in *The Oldest Old* (Suzman, Manton, & Wills, 1992). Other excellent sources are the MacArthur Foundation Study *Successful Aging* (Rowe & Kahn, 1998) and *Living to 100* (Perls & Silver, 1999). Taeuber and Rosenwaike (1992) use available census data to estimate that by the year 2010 there will be more than 6 million persons in the 85+ group, more than doubling the number in 1990. Moreover, whereas the total U.S. population has tripled since 1900, the number of people age 65+ has increased 11-fold. At the beginning of the 20th century, only 4% of people over 65 in the United States were over age 85; that figure currently exceeds 10% and is growing (Rowe & Kahn, 1998).

There is more limited information available on the really old, the centenarians. Much of the knowledge available about the U.S.

population aged 100 or more comes from the work of Poon and his colleagues in the Georgia Centenarian Study (1992) or from that of Perls and Wood (1999) in the New England Centenarian Study. Although very few persons over 100 existed in 1900, there are 61,000 currently over 100, and by 2050 the number is expected to reach 600,000 (Rowe & Kahn, 1998). Because this book focuses on those in their 80s and 90s, only passing references are made to those age 100 or more.

There are some demographic data available on those currently age 85 and over. These people are more predominantly female than any other age group, have more comorbidity, and are more apt to be institutionalized and to have limited education (Suzman et al., 1992). Currently there are only two men for every five women age 85 or more. Men are even more rare among those in their 90s and above; for instance, for those age 95 to 99, there were only 27 men for each 100 women in the 1990 census data.

It appears that the present oldest-old, those in their 80s, 90s, and 100s, are a group whose characteristics vary from those of younger elders, not only in their age but also in other demographic character-istics. Gender and race distinguish this special very old group from others more commonly identified as old. Moreover, these basic iden-tities have consequences for each in terms of lifestyle, function, and health, as well as overall quality of life.

MINORITY DATA

Blacks, on the other hand, are assuming a faster-growing proportion of the elderly than are whites (Richardson, 1992) and constituted 7.4% of the 85+ age cohort compared with less than 1% of the entire U.S. population of all ages in that category in 1990 (Taeuber & Rosenwaike, 1992), suggesting a longevity benefit for nonwhite el-derly. Indeed, expected mortality rates calculated on the basis of age fail to apply to those 85 and over and actually are below expected value for centenarians (Riggs & Millecchia, 1992). On the other hand, overall life expectancy is worse for blacks than for whites: White men live about 8 years longer than do blacks on the average, and white women about 6 years longer than their black counterparts (Rowe & Kahn, 1998).

LIFESTYLE

Lifestyle encompasses marital status, living arrangements, work, and leisure activities. There is virtually no nationwide information on these facets of lifestyle for those 85 and over. Marriage rates, as given in the 1997 *Statistical Abstract of the United States* (Bureau of the Census, 1997), are reported only for those aged 75+, revealing that in that age group 70% of men but only 27% of like-age women are currently married; whereas 41% live alone and 19% in nonfamily households. The gender disparity in marital status signals the fact that women suffer the death of a spouse more frequently than do men. Thus many women have to endure the loss of a major source of social support just when they need it most.

Employment information given in the census data is only for those 65 or older, who comprised almost 3% of the civilian labor force in 1996, with more men than women reported to be on the job. However, the median annual income of these workers was under $20,000, the lowest of any age group, and only 2.2% were in the top 5% of earners, lower than any age group except those age 15 to 24. Poverty status was given for those 75 and over, 13% of whom have income below the poverty level.

As for leisure activities, there are a few clues in the U.S. Census data. In 1995, only 4% at age 75+ spent money for reading and other entertainment. Of those age 75 to 96, 4% went to the movies, 7% to a sports event, and 14% to an amusement park at least once in the prior year. Also, 34% claimed to have been in exercise programs or done gardening in the previous 12 months. As for attendance at or participation in arts activity at least once over the prior year, among those 75 to 96, 10% visited museums or historic parks (Bureau of the Census, 1997). It is clear that even among some of the oldest-old, participation in relaxing activities is common. Missing, however, are data on travel for pleasure, which is not uncommon.

Rowe and Kahn (1998) pay considerable attention to what they call "continuing engagement with life," rejecting that retirement or old age constitutes a "roleless role." Counterpoised to the once-popular disengagement theory (in old age persons will not only relinquish their jobs, but also their recreations and interpersonal relations), successful aging implies continued engagement. For example, even the oldest-old can be both receivers and givers of social support, including emotional and practical, and continue to be productive in such activities as volunteer work in churches, hospitals, or childcare settings. Political volunteer work may be particularly attractive, because it involves social contacts in doing the many mailings, distributing leaflets, and phoning that political action requires. Home improvements can be a source of satisfying activity, as can giving aid of various kinds to both grandchildren and great grandchildren. Indeed, it is not uncommon for even the very old to boast that they are now busier than ever (Musil, 1998).

FUNCTIONAL ABILITY

There is considerable information on the functional ability of the oldest-old. Indeed, functional status is an issue in the relatively new discipline of "health expectancy" (Olshensky & Wilkins, 1998), the portion of life expectancy that is free of the burdens of functional loss and poor health. According to data from the *1992 Health Interview Survey* (National Center for Health Statistics, 1992), among those 85 and over, 22% suffer deficiencies in instrumental activities of daily living (IADL) and 20% have shortcomings in activities of daily living (ADL). Although there are some variations, generally IADLs include using the phone, going shopping, preparing meals, doing housework, taking medicine, and handling money, whereas ADLs concern the ability to eat, dress and undress, groom oneself, walk, get in and out of bed, take a bath or shower, and toileting. Seen positively, the *1992 Health Interview Survey* (Fowles, 1997x) revealed that 78 to 80% of the oldest-old have no difficulties with these everyday actions.

In the *1986 Health Interview Survey* (Van Nostrand, Furner, & Suzman, 1993), 35% of the men age 85 or more and 49% of the women had difficulties with ADLs, with walking and bathing the most common problem areas for both. As for IADLs, 65% of the women and 44% of the men had difficulties with three or more of these functions, most commonly shopping and housework for both genders. In the more recent AHEAD (asset and health dynamics among the oldest old) study (Rodgers & Miller, 1997), which sampled persons over 80, the mean number of ADLs with any limitation rose from less than one for those in their early 80s to two or more for respondents in their 90s. These statistics indicate that large numbers of the very old could still successfully undertake most or all of these activities, up to 60% without any limitations according to Van Nostrand et al. (1993).

One functional ability that is not covered in ADL and IADL studies is being able to drive an automobile. Loss of the right to drive a car seriously jeopardizes a person's independence and freedom of movement in the community. Yet, as shown by Sterns, Barrett, and Alexander (1985), the death rate by motor vehicle accidents for those age 75 and more is higher than that of any other driving age group except for teenagers and those in their early 20s. However, the findings do indicate a decline in driving accidents for those age 75 and over (Sterns et al., 1985), possibly reflecting a decision to avoid night driving and use of highways; in fact, death rates for motor vehicle accidents drop for those 85 and over (Sterns et al., 1985). Persuading an older person to give up the independence driving affords is one of the most difficult tasks faced by caregivers. Flunking a driving test usually settles the matter, but sometimes a more devious action may be needed, such as taking away the keys or disabling the car (Hunt, 1994).

PHYSICAL HEALTH

Facts on the comparative physical health of persons in their older years are available, and there is little need to belabor the point that physical ailments tend to increase with age. Unfortunately, however, much of the data do not cover those in their 80s and over, although 50% of persons 80 and over suffer from osteoporosis, a loss of bone density that can lead to fractures if the elder falls. Among men 75 years and older, 42% have arthritis, 11% have vision losses, 45% are hard of hearing, 12% have diabetes, 43% have heart conditions, and 34% have high blood pressure (selected from a total list of 24 chronic ailments). For women age 75+, the figures are 60% arthritis, 11% vision losses, 31% hard of hearing, 9% diabetes, 38% heart conditions, and 42% high blood pressure. In all cases except diabetes among women, these rates are higher than those reported for persons under 75 (Bureau of the Census, 1997). Once again, the flip sides of these figures indicate a significant number of persons who are free of these chronic conditions but unfortunately do not reveal the number who are free of all of them simultaneously.

These reports underscore the point that although chronic condition prevalence rises with age, the same is not necessarily true of various acute ailments, with the major exception of cancer. Although cancer is technically an acute condition different from ongoing ailments such as arthritis and heart ailments, it often requires extended treatment, which makes it similar to chronic illness in its impact. In fact, as death rates from heart disease and stroke decline, leaving more surviving into their 80s and beyond, cancer is likely to become the most common cause of mortality among the oldest-old (Rowe & Kahn, 1998). Declines in mortality rates in older ages are now being observed (Horichi & Wilmoth, 1998), however, while mortality rates accelerate in advanced ages for humans as well as other species (Vaupel, 1998).

Although use of health-care services such as hospitalizations and physician visits rises with age, with the most frequent usage recorded for those 65 and over, there are some unexpected variations among the oldest-old. One recent study of health-care expenditures in Massachusetts (Perls & Wood, 1996) found that hospital costs actually declined among those 90 and older, compared with the younger old, those 70 to 79, whose hospital charges were the highest. This was partly due to differences in the type of problem presented and partly to the preponderance of care for the oldest in nonteaching hospitals.

Physical decline because of the aging of muscular strength known as sarcopenia is a continuous process beginning in middle age but worsening in later years. Persons aged 75 or 80 who have been sedentary have lost not only muscle strength but also lung capacity. According to Rowe and Kahn (1998), just taking a shower may use up to half of the strength of persons who have been sedentary all their lives. Women are particularly affected. Women in this age group have only 80% of the aerobic capacity of like-age men. Unfortunately, although regular exercise could slow or even reverse many losses, less than one in five of those 75 or over engage in such activity. Both aerobic exercise and weight lifting could benefit even the very old, in many cases even doubling their endurance after less than a year of regular physical activity (Rowe & Kahn, 1998). Exercise of both types has been found to reduce the incidence of heart disease and hypertension, cut the risk of diabetes and stroke, and even relieve arthritis (Rowe & Kahn, 1998) in the oldest-old, yet disability may accumulate with diminished activity (Vita, Terry, Hebert, & Fries, 1998).

Finally, the very old are apt to be optimistic about their health. In one report on self-assessed health by age group, 35% of those 85 and over considered their health excellent or very good, slightly more than those 75+, with the women a bit more sanguine than the men were (Mermelstein, Miller, Prohaska, Benson, & Van Nostrand, 1993).

MENTAL HEALTH

The mental and emotional situations of the very old have not been studied very extensively. Census data are nonexistent. Major studies in earlier years, such as those summarized by Blazer (1983), only covered elderly aged 65+ without differentiating those in their 80s and 90s. The book by Suzman et al. (1992) on the oldest-old does not cover mental health at all. One clue to mental illness in the aged might be derived from suicide rates, because data are given on rates for those 85 and over (Bureau of the Census, 1995). Rates are consistently the lowest for those 85 and over (at 0.7 to 0.1) for both men and women and for both blacks and whites. Because the highest rates occur among the middle aged, it is possible that the most suicidal die before they reach old age, leaving the survivors least likely to take their own lives.

One major source of data is the centenarian studies of Poon et al. (1992) in Georgia, where they examined various mental health factors of those 60 to 79 and 80 to 89, as well as of those in their 100s. Comparing these three groups according to the six indicators of mental health in the Older Americans Resources and Services (OARS) survey (Fillenbaum, 1988), Poon and his colleagues found significant and substantial differences by age group. The most marked age differences were found in feeling useless, a negative mental health attitude claimed by only 21% of the young old and 28% of those in their 80s but 56% of the centenarians; a similar pattern applied to feeling weak. Unexpectedly, well over 90% of all three groups denied ever feeling lonely, considering that in another section of the OARS instrument, on social support, 29% and 27% of the two younger cohorts and 42% of the very oldest admitted to feeling lonely sometimes or often. Perhaps in the context of talking about seeing or visiting friends and family as part of the social support inquiry, the realization of the loss of such contacts reminded respondents about feeling alone. As Kahn and Antonucci (1980) have pointed out, decline in the number of people in one's social circle because of moving away, death, and institutionalization is one of the critical losses suffered by the very old, leading to diminished social contacts and loneliness (Bonderik & Stogstad, 1998). An unexpected finding in the MacArthur Foundation studies was that higher mental function was likely to be related to better physical function, which in turn was enhanced by the frequency of emotional support but not practical support. In one project, subjects who averaged in the mid-70s in age, were followed for 8 years, into their 80s. At that time, of those who had earlier enjoyed both adequate physical function and good emotional support, more than half maintained their level of functioning, and almost a quarter actually improved as they aged (Rowe & Kahn, 1998).

DEPRESSION, ANXIETY, AND DEMENTIA

Depression and anxiety are two mental health complaints that are supposedly common among many very old people. Again, finding data that relate to depression and the oldest ages presents some difficulties. In a study that assessed the propensity of community-dwelling elders to interpret a bodily change as an illness, the relationship between those whose age was less than 80 and those 80 and over with depressive symptomology was evaluated (Haug, 1995). Based on the CESD (Center for the Epidemiological Study of Depression) scale created by the National Institute of Mental Health (NIMH) to assess depression symptoms in community populations, the very old are quite similar to the younger old in their likelihood of clinical depression, both being in the 14 to 15% range for such a diagnosis.

The Atlanta Centenarian Study data also showed very little variation in emotional stability among those age 80+ and only small differences among the three age categories studied (Adkins, Martin, & Poon, 1996). In a sample of rural women in Nebraska, 91% of those age 75 to 84 years and 86% of those age 85 to 94 years suffered moderate to high depressive symptoms (Craft, Johnson, & Ortega, 1998). However, as George (1993) points out, older persons may be afflicted by depressive symptoms that fail to meet the psychiatric definitions of a depressive disorder or have depressive syndromes that do not fit diagnostic criteria. Moreover, because studies of the oldest-old are so rare, little is known of the applicability of common methods of mental health measurement to those over 80.

The findings about anxiety among the elderly are compatible with those on depression. In the Atlanta Centenarian Study, anxiety rates varied only marginally across the three age cohorts (Adkins et al., 1996). However, the method of measurement used did not fit the seven types of anxiety in official psychiatric diagnosis, and the scarce data on anxiety that exist in other research are not differentiated by age level (Gurian & Goisman, 1993). Although the common conclusion is that both depression and anxiety do not worsen among the elderly, their incidence and prevalence among the oldest-old have not yet been adequately established.

Dementia, or cognitive impairment, is known to increase with age, reaching its highest prevalence among centenarians (Smith, 1997). Although it is not often classified with mental illness, cognitive impairment certainly has a negative impact on quality of life similar to that of other mental complaints. A decrease in cognitive function among the very old is not necessarily related to functional impairment, however (Corey-Bloom, Wilderholt, Edelstein, & Salmon, 1996). Occurrence of the dementia defined as Alzheimer's disease (AD), omitting that due to cardiovascular accidents, has been estimated by the meta-analysis of 18 studies by the U.S. General Accounting Office (1998) for the Secretary of Health and Human Services (GAO/HEHS-98-16). This analysis estimated that the rate for all severity levels of AD for men ranged from 5.6 at age 80 to 35.6 at age 95; for women, the rate ranged from 7.1 to 41.5 for the same age categories.

Clearly, this loss of cognitive function and mental activity can be a severe health problem for persons of advanced years. Some (particularly those who are physically fit and have more years of education and higher income) are more apt to retain their cognitive capacities. The speed of memory recall and the type of memory being accessed are both affected in the later years. Speed of remembering is slower, and some types of recall, "explicit memory," are impaired. The power to bring to mind a familiar name, number, or word is lessened in the very old and thus is probably caused by changes brought about by age itself. However, better education, physical health, and a sense of mastery or belief in one's self-efficacy can minimize these age effects and assist in limiting cognitive impairment, even in the oldest-old (Rowe & Kahn, 1998).

MINORITY DIFFERENCES

Information on differences in health and function among the very old by minority status is difficult to find. The crossover effect (the age at which death rates in whites exceed those of blacks) has generated some controversy about its accuracy without defining any possible reasons for its occurrence. One epidemiology study based on Medicare records concluded that the crossover in 1987 data occurred at age 86 for men and 88 for women. As indicated earlier in this chapter, the number of black aged is growing more rapidly than that of aged whites, findings also noted by Jackson (1988). Yet, knowledge of the characteristics of the oldest old Blacks is not readily available. Gibson and Jackson (1992), however, have noted that blacks age 85 and over are similar to their white counterparts in chronic conditions and problems with ADLs. These data are based on the 1984 *Supplement on Aging of the National Health Interview Survey* in which the number of blacks aged 85+ was small. One intriguing conclusion of Gibson and Jackson (1992) was that the relationships between various health measures and age are linear for whites but are nonlinear for blacks, with the 85-and-over group less ill and disabled than those 80 to 84.

QUALITY OF LIFE

Lifestyles, functional ability, and physical and mental health all combine to contribute to an overall quality of life, but that concept includes more. As suggested by Spitzer (1980) and others, in addition to health, good quality of life covers factors such as independence in being able to take care of oneself; various useful kinds of productive activity, whether paid or volunteer; the support of others in one's everyday endeavors; and a positive outlook on life, particularly of the future. This is an abbreviated version of the definition given by Stewart and King (1991) but seems adequate for the purpose of this book (Abeles, Gift, & Ory, 1994). Independence in being able to take care of oneself has been implied earlier in this chapter in connection with ADL and IADL, for which 78 to 80% of the oldest-old were reported to have no difficulties with these activities. But there are three levels of difficulty, including a level of being able to perform the activity "with help." Help, depending on how it is defined, can be consistent with independence. For example, using a cane or motorscooter can offer freedom of movement, even for persons with severe physical impairment. The blind can live independently with the aid of a seeing-eye dog or specially constructed kitchen or bathroom equipment, or both. Persons who can no longer drive to a supermarket or shopping center can arrange for special transportation or even order by phone.

In short, independence does not require perfection or solo performance in either mobility or home duties, and the very old who have found ways to secure some assistance in daily living can maintain considerable independence in taking care of their needs. Furthermore, the two facets of ADLs are highly correlated. The very old who do very well in ADL are apt to be proficient in IADL as well.

Engaging in productive activities is another critical component of a positive quality of life. Here, the MacArthur Foundation studies have much to contribute. In an entire chapter on productivity in old age, Rowe and Kahn (1998) start by defining the concept as "any activity, paid or unpaid that generates goods or services of economic value" (p. 169). This definition includes any kind of regular housework—meal preparation, cleaning, shopping—as well as house maintenance and home improvement tasks. Another productive activity is providing aid, both emotional and practical, to friends, neighbors, and relatives. Then there is the plethora of volunteer work, already alluded to, in organizations of all kinds: schools, churches, hospitals, political groups, and movements to improve the environment. Not all work is voluntary. Some very old persons, particularly those in the arts or professions, may continue to draw a paycheck well into their 80s. As Rowe and Kahn point out (1998), having a higher education is linked to productivity in old age. As of 1996, 13% of those age 75+ had at least a bachelor's degree, and some had postgraduate degrees.

It is worth noting that education not only offers access to nonroutine, more interesting professional work but also offers an independent contribution to quality of life. It provides better access to economic resources. In 1994 data (Bureau of the Census, 1994), persons 65 and over who are college graduates earned more than twice the dollars of a non–high school–educated elder, and those with postgraduate degrees nearly six times more. In addition, education may contribute to an old person's sense of mastery and control over life events. It may enhance marital stability and more widespread social contacts that offer a variety of opportunities for social support. In these aspects, at least, education can be viewed as contributing to better quality of life (Ross & Van Willigen, 1997).

This contribution is apt to be relevant only to the minority of those in their 80s and 90s who were fortunate enough to acquire a higher education. Seventy or 80 years ago when those who are very old now were in their teens, even completing high school was an achievement, and large numbers were forced to go to work after completing 8th grade or even earlier. Although many enriched their lives with continuing informal learning, access to the types of productive activity available to those with higher academic degrees was beyond their grasp. Thus, the quality of life associated with productive activity may not really be a condition of their existence.

Furthermore, the benefits of higher education are undoubtedly only germane to the small minority of men among the oldest-old. Girls had little or no opportunity for more years of schooling in the early part of the 20th century, and women constitute the large majority of those still living today.

Still another contribution to positive quality of life is having satisfactory relationships with others. In earlier years a large proportion of social friendships arise in the workplace; in the older years, such relationships can flower in connection with volunteer work, as well as membership in social clubs, political parties, church groups, and "cause" organizations such as those interested in improving the environment of the neighborhood or the planet. All can offer multiple chances for new, close friendships. Unfortunately, one major source of social support, that of a spouse in a marital relationship, is largely denied to the very old, particularly women. The dearth of men among those in their 80s and 90s makes the support of a spouse unavailable for most old women.

Contrary to popular belief, many old women also miss the sexual relations that a male partner can supply. The male/female disparity becomes in many ways a major reason for diminished quality of life among the oldest-old. Also, the sexual potency of men usually declines in old age, and for both genders sexual interest can diminish because of chronic illness or use of medication. However, the dearth of partners is not as common a problem for men as for women, and new medications such as Viagra® are available to correct some shortcomings in performance. Lack of a major component of social support is accordingly a common ground for lower quality of life, predominantly for old women.

In analyzing social support, Antonucci (1986) and Kahn and Antonucci (1980) developed the concept of *convoy*, concentric circles of support around an individual from the most intimate inner ring to the outer ring of most casual and most distant. The major intimate support in the convoy is that received from the spouse, whose absence among the oldest-old has already been discussed. The next rings in the convoy consist of children, close friends, coworkers, and neighbors. Among the oldest-old, these are diminished because children may die in their 60s or move too far away to be a ready or convenient source of support for a parent in her 90s or 100s. Similarly, close friends die or move away to be with their children or are no longer easily available for other reasons, such as frailty or institutionalization. Former coworkers who are still living no longer have mutual work interests with their prior colleagues and drift away. The oldest-old move to living arrangements more convenient for their needs and lose contact with old neighbors, who also may have changed residences.

An outer ring of the convoy may include familiar shopkeepers, clerks, or professionals, all subject to many changes. The old drugstore has become part of a mammoth chain; the helpful grocery clerks of an earlier time have disappeared into a supermarket. The hairdresser who knew just how the old lady wanted her hair done has retired, and the substitute cannot equal the predecessor. Because in middle age many have physicians who are older than they are, in later years these physicians die or retire, leaving the people who outlive them in need of finding someone new, with all the communication difficulties that implies (Haug, 1988). In other words, living into one's 80s, 90s, or more guarantees changes in all levels of social support. Continuity of social support, if it exists at all, is usually rare. Again, the costs will fall most heavily on very old women, the majority of the oldest-old.

The concept of a positive outlook on life as a major component of life quality implies the absence of depression among the oldest-old, yet virtually no attention to this admittedly common problem is offered in Rowe and Kahn (1998). In a review of mental disorders, Dohrenwend (1983) pointed out that clinical depression is most common in women and is often directly related to environmentally induced stress, with recent life events that involve loss a particularly significant stressor that may lead to depression. As data already presented definitely indicate, these circumstances are characteristic of the oldest-old. Most are women, many of whom have frailties that make the mastery of their living environments problematic, and all of whom, because of their longevity, have lost many friends and family members, particularly spouses, through earlier death.

On the other hand, lowered mood should be distinguished from clinical depression. A historical and cultural overview of the ailment (Shorter, 1993) reminds us that clinical depression is both a biological and a cultural phenomenon, the treatment and diagnosis of which has varied widely over the years. It is probable that lowered mood rather than clinical depression is the most common complaint among the very old. Indeed, George (1993) has suggested that measurement among all elderly by the usual depression scales may be off the mark on the grounds that manifestations of depression will be different in persons of advanced ages. Without a study of the mental health well-being of the oldest-old, any conclusion must technically remain speculative, but the likelihood of widespread lowered mood at least fits the known data remarkably well.

One final factor in quality of life is a positive outlook toward the future, involving plans for pleasurable activities as well as rejecting a focus on mortality. Although Rowe and Kahn (1998) are persistently upbeat, they have no references to either negative or positive planning for the future. Death is only mentioned twice and then as "premature." Data on death rates are given but only as evidence for current and future longevity trends. Weil, in his book *Spontaneous*

Healing (1997), is at least more realistic, giving examples of planning for the future that do not evade death as an outcome but actually specify steps for putting one's affairs in order and limiting trauma and after-death tasks for the survivors. The inevitability of demise, however, need not forestall plans for travel, visiting, or other pleasurable activities. Given the suggested possible life span of 120 years, even 100-year-old people with a positive perspective can formulate agendas for fun things to do in the coming months, if not necessarily the coming years, of their lives. These aged can enjoy a satisfactory, even pleasurable, quality of life that they can project into the 21st century.

COHORT CHANGES

Issues of lifestyle, function, physical health, mental well-being, and overall quality of life among the oldest-old have been addressed briefly in this chapter. The reader must remember, however, that none of these results may apply to those in other countries who turn 85 and over during the 21st century. Moreover, cohorts (groups of people born during the same 10- or 20-year period) have similar experiences or exposure to events during their lifetimes. Those age 80 to 100 in 1990 were born in the period from 1890 to 1910, before many modern appliances were invented or important discoveries were made in treatments for illness. They experienced two world wars along with a technology expansion unlike anything that has happened before, including massive changes in air and automobile travel as well as the fact that television and computers are now common household items. Future cohorts, such as the baby boomers born at the end of World War II, will have had entirely different experiences, beliefs, and attitudes that will affect their lives as persons in their 80s and older. The findings in this book are therefore time bound. As fascinating as they may be, the reader must remember that they represent only a slice of time and must be cautious about applying them too far into the future.

What the findings do offer, nevertheless, is a capsule image of the social context in which the activities and experiences of the subjects, whose stories will be told in the balance of the book, actually occurred. That context is critical in evaluating this empirical study of a sample of the oldest-old in a Midwestern city.

CHAPTER 2

The Lives of the Oldest Old in Everyday Focus

Although persons aged 85 or older who live in the community are small in absolute numbers, this old-old age group has been growing at a rate almost three times faster than that for those age 65 to 84 (Grundy, 1997). There have been few longitudinal studies of the oldest-old, and other cross-sectional studies have included very small numbers in this age group. Although a few studies have included the oldest-old (Bould, Sanborn, & Reif, 1989; Poon, Clayton, et al., 1992; Rowe & Kahn, 1998), little is really known about the very old and their circumstances.

At least 40% of persons 85 or older need help from another person to carry out ADLs, but many remain active and independent (Van Nostrand, Furner, & Suzman, 1993). To remain in the community, the oldest-old must be independent in performing tasks related to personal care (ADLs) and those related to caring for the home and engaging in activities outside the home (IADLs). Elderly adults with dependence in IADLs and some ADLs more frequently receive informal care from friends and family, as well as formal services (Hing & Bloom, 1990). With higher rates of dependence, the rates of institutionalization and death rise (Hirsch, Sommers, Olsen, Mullen, & Winograd, 1991; Manton, 1988).

Although the risks of chronic disease accelerate rapidly with advancing age, they are not evenly distributed among the oldest-old and do not uniformly result in dependency in daily activities (Nagi, 1991). Factors that disrupt normal processes may lead to psychological and physical abnormalities (Nagi, 1991). These aberrations interfere with the performance of daily activities (e.g., inability to rise from a chair or pick up a penny from the floor). Subsequently, these functional limitations can lead to disability for which ADLs and IADLs are components (Roberts, 1999). Deteriorating health and increasing disability may present the oldest-old with chronic strains, necessitating, at times, the development of new coping strategies.

Physical and cognitive factors associated with independence in daily activities have been well-studied (Roberts, 1999), but the stressors (life events) and worries (daily hassles) experienced by the very old are not well-known. For the very old, changes rooted in physical, emotional, and social losses are apt to be frequent occurrences, requiring an ability to adjust and reintegrate goals and self-esteem. The coping strategies and resources for dealing with stress that may have once been effective may no longer be adequate to deal with chronic stresses and worries associated with deteriorating health, increasing disability, and substantive changes in the social network. The stresses and worries and the effectiveness of coping strategies and resources may affect lifestyles of the oldest-old as well as beliefs about themselves. Moreover, how elderly adults appraise stressors and worries and coping resources may affect the decisions they make about what and how they perform daily activities (Roberts, 1999) and whether they are able to live independently or need to relocate to a family member's home or an assisted living or long-term care facility.

Although there are an enormous number of studies of stress, coping, and coping resources, few focus on those 85 of age and older. Data from the present longitudinal study provide greater insight into these issues. This chapter focuses on the condition and circumstances of the very old and compares those subjects who did not survive past the first interview with those who survived to Wave 4, 18 months later, and Wave 5, 9 years from the first interview. Enough time elapsed between these data points that change was possible.

BRIEF DESCRIPTION OF SAMPLE

Respondents who were interviewed at Wave 1 only are referred to as nonsurvivors. Those who lived to Wave 4 but not Wave 5 are referred to as Wave 4 survivors, and those living to the last interview are referred to as Wave 5 survivors. Findings for each of these three subgroups are presented in Table 2.1.

Although comparisons of findings among all three of the subgroups could be made, there were very few statistically significant differences, and these are not highlighted in the discussion following. Nonetheless, post hoc tests of comparisons using least squares difference (LSD) among the three subgroups revealed a few significant differences in those who did not survive to Wave 4. Although differences among the three groups were negligible, nonsurvivors were significantly younger ($M = 87.1$ years) than were those whose last interview was Wave 4 ($M = 88.1$ years; $LSD = -0.99$, $p < 0.05$) but not significantly older than Wave 5 survivors ($M = 86.6$ years). The nonsurvivors were significantly more dependent in IADLs ($M = 11.3$) than were those completing the 9-year study ($M = 13.1$; $LSD = -1.81$, $p < 0.001$) but not significantly more dependent than those last interviewed at Wave 4 ($M = 11.9$). The nonsurvivors had significantly lower ratings of health ($M = 1.50$) than had Wave 4 survivors ($M = 1.83$; $LSD = -0.33$, $p < 0.02$) and those completing the last interview ($M = 1.91$). Although the nonsurvivors had significantly poorer ratings of health than the two other subgroups had, the differences in ratings were negligible and are of no practical significance.

MENTAL HEALTH

Although physical health is an important contributor to mental health at any age, mental health has been shown to contribute to longevity (Pitskhelauri, 1983) and has been conceptualized as an important adaptational factor in the oldest old (Poon, Martin, Clayton, Messner, Noble, & Johnson, 1992; Poon, Clayton, et al., 1992).

Between 73% and 80% of respondents rated their mental health as good to excellent, and no significant differences in these ratings occurred across time points. Although nearly 53% of Wave 5 survivors rated their mental health as excellent, only 30% of those completing

TABLE 2.1   Description of Variables by Interview for Respondents Last Interviewed at Wave 4 and Those Surviving to the Last Interview, 9 Years After Baseline

Variable	Wave 1		Wave 4		Wave 5
	Survived to Wave 4 but not to Wave 5 $(n = 131)^*$	Survived to Wave 5 $(n = 23)$	Survived to Wave 4 but not to Wave 5 $(n = 131)$	Survived to Wave 5 $(n = 23)$	Survived to Wave 5 $(n = 23)$
Stressors					
Negative (theoretical range 0–24)	$2.3^\dagger$ $(1.5)^\ddagger$	2.0 (1.5)	2.0 (1.4)	2.2 (1.6)	—§
Positive (theoretical range 0–5)	0.6 (0.8)	0.08 (0.8)	0.87 (0.9)	0.78 (0.7)	—
Worry (theoretical range 0–46)	7.5 (6.4)	6.1 (6.7)	11.3 (9.5)	8.4 (8.3)	27.0 (6.7)
Problem-Focused Coping (theoretical range 0–6; higher score more problem-focused coping)	2.1 (1.5)	2.0 (1.6)	2.9 (1.6)	2.7 (1.4)	—
Mental Health					
Self-rated mental health (theoretical range 0–3)	2.1 (0.7)	2.4 (0.7)	1.9 (0.7)	2.4 (0.7)	2.0 (0.8)
Compared with others (theoretical range 0–3)	1.7 (0.5)	1.7 (0.5)	1.6 (0.5)	1.7 (0.5)	—
Compared with 5 years ago (6 months for Waves 4) (theoretical range 0–3)	1.7 (0.6)	1.8 (0.8)	0.93 (0.4)	2.0 (0.7)	—
Depression (theoretical range 0–24)	2.3 (2.9)	1.1 (1.7)	3.2 (3.9)	1.7 (2.5)	3.6 (4.3)
Affect balance (theoretical range 0–10)	6.9 (2.1)	7.1 (1.8)	6.5 (2.2)	7.0 (1.3)	6.7 (2.1)

TABLE 2.1 *(continued)*

Variable	Wave 1		Wave 4		Wave 5
	Survived to Wave 4 but not to Wave 5 $(n = 131)^*$	Survived to Wave 5 $(n = 23)$	Survived to Wave 4 but not to Wave 5 $(n = 131)$	Survived to Wave 5 $(n = 23)$	Survived to Wave 5 $(n = 23)$
Physical Health					
Self-rated health (theoretical range 0–3)	1.8 (0.8)	1.9 (0.6)	1.6 (0.8)	1.9 (0.8)	1.6 (0.7)
Compared with others (theoretical range 0–3)	2.6 (0.6)	2.8 (0.4)	2.6 (0.5)	2.8 (0.4)	—
Compared with 5 years ago (6 months for Wave 4) (theoretical range 0–3)	1.7 (0.6)	1.8 (0.8)	1.8 (0.6)	2.0 (0.7)	—
Activities of Daily Living					
Physical ADL§ (theoretical range 0–12)	11.4 (0.8)	11.7 (0.5)	11.3 (1.0)	11.5 (1.1)	10.3 (2.4)
IADL (theoretical range 0–14)	11.9 (2.0)	13.1 (1.2)	11.3 (2.5)	13.2 (1.2)	8.9 (3.5)
Self-esteem (theoretical range 1–20)	11.3 (3.3)	13.0 (4.2)	10.1 (3.6)	13.2 (3.3)	13.3 (2.9)
Social Support					
Availability of assistance (theoretical range 0–4)	4.0 (1.0)	4.1 (1.0)	4.1 (1.1)	4.3 (0.9)	4.2 (0.9)
Frequency of social interaction (theoretical range 0–9)	9.6 (1.8)	10.0 (1.5)	9.4 (2.1)	9.7 (2.1)	9.4 (2.3)

(continued)

TABLE 2.1   *(continued)*

Variable	Wave 1		Wave 4		Wave 5
	Survived to Wave 4 but not to Wave 5 $(n = 131)^*$	Survived to Wave 5 $(n = 23)$	Survived to Wave 4 but not to Wave 5 $(n = 131)$	Survived to Wave 5 $(n = 23)$	Survived to Wave 5 $(n = 23)$
Mastery					
Global perceived control (theoretical range 0–12)	5.8 (2.5)	6.4 (2.8)	6.4 (3.0)	6.4 (2.9)	6.3 (2.6)
Perceived control of events (theoretical range 0–3)	2.2 (0.7)	2.3 (0.9)	2.0 (1.1)	2.5 (0.9)	1.9 (1.1)

[*]Subjects who were interviewed at Wave 4 but not at Wave 5
[†]Mean
[‡]Standard deviation
[§]Not measured at Wave 5

Wave 4 rated their mental health this way. In contrast, a greater proportion of Wave 4 survivors rated their mental health as good (56.6%) than did those completing the last interview (39.1%). At all time points and for both groups of respondents, nearly 80% indicated that their mental health was the same as it was earlier. Between 60 and 70% rated their mental health at all five interviews as better than others their own age and nearly 70% of Wave 4 and Wave 5 survivors rated their mental health similarly.

Across all five interviews, there were no significant gender or racial differences in ratings of mental health. In contrast, others found that blacks had significantly lower mental health ratings than did their white counterparts (Kim, Bramlett, Wright, & Poon, 1998). However, they did not separate the oldest-old in their analyses, which may account for the inconsistency in findings.

The ratings of mental health were consistent with a measure of good mental health, the Affect Balance Scale (Bradburn, 1969), for which the means ranged from 6.6 to 7.1 out of a maximum score of 10. This measure of mental health also remained stable across all five waves of interviews, and mental health for Wave 4 survivors was similar to that of respondents who completed the last interview 9 years after the baseline interview. No gender or racial differences were found.

Depression was low, with means ranging from 2.1 to 3.6 on a scale of 0 to 24, but it did increase slightly over time, as did its variability. However, Wave 5 survivors were significantly less depressed at baseline and Wave 4 ($M = 1.1$ and 1.7, respectively) than were Wave 4 survivors ($M = 2.3$ and 3.2, respectively). Nearly 70% of Wave 4 and Wave 5 survivors had no symptoms of depression (score of 0) at the first interview. This proportion dropped to 63% for Wave 4 survivors at Wave 4 but increased to 83% at Wave 5. In spite of these feelings, more than 90% of subjects across all time points reported no thoughts of ending their life. Although these findings are inconsistent with those of others (Kim et al., 1998), these investigators did not perform subgroup analyses with the oldest-old, and they used different measurement strategies for mental health than were used in our study.

As for the other measures of mental health, there were no significant racial and gender differences in depression or thoughts about suicide. Since blacks living into their mid-80s survive most of their counterparts and may be healthier (Rowe & Kahn, 1998), racial differences may not be evident in the very old.

PHYSICAL HEALTH

Although there is consensus that physical health declines with age, data specifically related to those over 85 years are lacking. In our study, only two respondents had no chronic conditions. The most frequent chronic conditions experienced by the oldest-old respondents were vision problems (97%), arthritis (65%), hearing problems (56%), hypertension (32%), and cardiac disease (26%). As found by others (Gibson & Jackson, 1992), the proportion of these chronic conditions was not significantly different between white and black respondents. Except for hypertension, all these chronic conditions may have a significant impact on mobility and independence in ADLs.

Compared with men, women had more chronic diseases, which is similar to the findings of others (Guralnik & Simonsick, 1993). Compared with men, more women had hypertension (15% and 38%, respectively), cardiac disease (17% and 28%, respectively), and arthritis (52% and 69%, respectively). Almost all men and women experienced vision problems (97%), whereas more men experienced difficulties with hearing (67% and 53%, respectively). The proportion of respondents with these diseases was greater than in a national sample of persons over 75 years of age (Bureau of the Census, 1997). For men in the census data, 42% had arthritis, 11% had vision problems, 45% had hearing impairments, 43% had heart disease, and 34% had hypertension. Since chronic disease increases with age, it is not surprising that the proportion of respondents with these diseases was greater than in a national sample in which the sample included younger elders from the ages of 75 to 84 years.

Although no statistically significant gender differences in chronic conditions were found, significantly more men than women died during the first 18 months of our study (23.9% and 7.5%, respectively; $\chi^2 = 9.44$, $p < 0.01$). The gender differences in mortality are not surprising because the census data reveal that the proportion of men drops precipitously with very advanced age (Bureau of the Census, 1997).

Similar to others (Gibson & Jackson, 1992), there were no racial differences in the proportion of respondents with these chronic conditions or in mortality during the first 18 months among blacks and their white counterparts (17.6% and 10.1%, respectively). The lack of significant racial differences in mortality may be explained by the fact that blacks living into their mid-80s have survived most of their black counterparts and may be healthier and less likely to die than are white adults of similar age (Rowe & Kahn, 1998).

In spite of the high prevalence of chronic disease in our study, 85 to 90% of the respondents rated their health as good to excellent at Waves 1 to 4. However, a smaller proportion of Wave 5 (13%) survivors rated their health as excellent compared with Wave 4 survivors (20.8%). In contrast, at the Wave 4 interview, a greater proportion of respondents completing all 9 years of our study (21.7%) rated their health as excellent than did Wave 4 survivors (12.2%). By the last interview, only 8.7% rated their health as excellent; equal percentages rated it as good and fair (43.5%). Whether these ratings of health represent changes in health status is unknown.

We do know that health problems limited the activities of these very old respondents. At the baseline interview, more than 65% of those completing the entire study stated that their health did not prevent them from doing things, whereas only 13% indicated that it interfered a great deal. In contrast, 41.5% of Wave 4 survivors stated that health prevented them from doing things, and nearly 24% indicated that it interfered a great deal. At Wave 4, these percentages remained nearly the same for both groups. The proportion stating that health interfered a great deal with activities remained stable from the baseline interview to Wave 4, at 20% for Wave 4 survivors and 15% for those completing the last interview. Clearly, those surviving the entire 9 years of our study believed that health interfered little with activities, whereas those who did not live to the last interview were more affected by their health. By the last interview, however, the proportion of respondents that believed this was true was only 22%, and 44% stated that health problems interfered with activities a great deal.

Physical capabilities influence the performance of daily activities. At Wave 4, the degree to which health interfered with activities was associated with less independence in ADL for survivors of Wave 4 ($r = -0.48$) and Wave 5 ($r = -0.36$). Stronger negative relationships were found between independence in IADL and interference with activities in Wave 5 survivors ($r = -0.74$) than in Wave 4 survivors ($r = -0.28$). These findings add support to beliefs that the adverse effects of health are reflected in lessened independence in daily activities. Whether these perceptions were consistent with physical abilities or influence the decisions about daily activities of the very old was not possible to determine in our study.

No statistically significant racial or gender differences were found for perceptions of health and its influence on the performance of activities. These findings are inconsistent with other studies (Ford, Haug, Jones, & Folmar, 1990; Kim et al., 1998) that included respondents 60 and over. This inconsistency may reflect the cross-over in survival that is known to occur at approximately 85 years of age for black women (Jackson, 1988). Those who survived to be included in our study may have been healthier than younger participants were in other studies (Ford, Haug, Roy, & Folkman, 1992; Gibson & Jackson, 1992; Kim et al., 1998).

Data regarding nursing home and hospital stays corroborate the finding that respondents in our study were healthy in spite of the high prevalence of chronic disease. Only 2 had a stay in a nursing home, and only 26 (13%) were hospitalized in the 6 months prior to the first interview. These proportions were similar among those that survived only to the Wave 4 interview as well as respondents completing the entire 9 years of our study. Similar proportions of whites and blacks had hospital and nursing home stays at all time points, findings inconsistent with others who reported that more blacks were hospitalized (Ford et al., 1990). Moreover, more than 85% of male and female respondents did not have a hospital or a nursing home stay within 6 months of the interview for all five waves of data collection.

Although hospitalizations and nursing home stays were low in our study, 80% had reported seeing a physician one to three times during each of the interviews. These results are consistent with information about outpatient visits in the 1995 census data (Bureau of the Census, 1997) in which the average number of visits for a year by persons over 75 years of age was six. Although only 8.7% of respondents completing our study had not seen a physician in the previous 6 months, more than 21% of Wave 4 survivors indicated as such. A greater proportion of those completing Wave 5 had seen a physician one to three times in 6 months (78.0%) than had Wave 4 survivors (37.3%). This was surprising because Wave 5 survivors had perceptions of better health than Wave 4 survivors had. Perhaps those completing the entire study were more responsive to health changes and sought out health care sooner than did Wave 4 survivors. They also may have engaged in more healthful behaviors and, hence, may have been more likely to survive the entire 9 years. Findings of our study support this hypothesis to some extent because a greater proportion of those who lived to the last interview exercised sometimes or often (43.7%) as compared with Wave 4 survivors (32.9%). Whether these respondents engaged in exercise to improve health or for pleasure it is unknown. Regardless, these are all hypotheses that require further study.

FUNCTIONAL ABILITY

Although disability increases with comorbidity (Bould et al., 1988; Guralnik & Simonsick, 1993), they are not the same (Ford et al., 1990). Disability is related to poor functional ability in the performance of tasks and is central to health expectancy theory (Olshensky & Wilkins, 1998) that focuses on the portion of life free of poor health and functional impairment. Because functioning is negatively related to age, those 85 years of age or older have significantly greater limitations than do younger adults (Guralnik & Simonsick, 1993; Parker, Thorslund, & Nordstrom, 1992), with approximately one third of the oldest-old having significant disabilities (Parker et al., 1992; Zarit, Johansson, & Malmberg, 1995). The declines in health and increases in disability may contribute to dependence in daily activities, which may be more salient to the lives of the very old.

The findings from our study can be compared with those from the 1992 Health Interview Survey of persons 85 and older. In that study, 22% were dependent in at least one IADL and 20% in at least one ADL (Fowles, 1998). Others found that 80% required assistance with at least one of these activities (Coroni-Huntley et al., 1992). In our study, dependency in at least one ADL was greater than 40% at Waves 1 and 4. Dependency in IADLs was 74% at Wave 1 and 71% at Wave 4. In contrast, at Wave 5, only one respondent was independent in all IADLs, whereas only nine respondents were independent in all ADLs. These findings are similar to those found by some (Van Nostrand et al., 1993) but higher than found by others (Coroni-Huntley et al., 1992; Fowles, 1998).

At the baseline interview, a greater proportion of Wave 5 survivors were independent in all IADLs (78.3%) than were Wave 4 survivors (24.4%). Yet, similar proportions were independent in all ADLs (58%). At Wave 4, 78% of Wave 5 survivors were independent in all ADLs, whereas 70% of Wave 4 survivors were independent. Similar findings at Wave 4 were found for IADL, for which 78% of Wave 5 survivors and 61% of Wave 4 survivors were independent.

Similarly, at the baseline interview, the differences in the total ADLs were small between those living to the last interview and Wave 4 survivors ($M = 11.74$ and 11.41, respectively). In contrast, Wave 5 survivors ($M = 13.13$) were significantly more independent in IADLs than were Wave 4 survivors (11.92; t [152] = −4.06, p < 0.001). These differences remained significant at the Wave 4 interview (M = 11.29 for Wave 4 survivors and 13.22 for Wave 5 survivors; t [151] = −5.94, p < 0.001). Perhaps, Wave 4 survivors had already experienced a decline in independence in these activities whereas those who lived to Wave 5 may have just begun to experience such a decline. Other prospective studies are needed to assess this hypothesis.

In the Health Interview Survey (Fowles, 1998), 35% of men and 44% of women 85 and older had dependencies in ADLs, and 44% of men and 65% of women were dependent in IADLs. In our study, 37% of men and 42% of women had difficulties with ADLs at Wave 1, and the proportions changed little by Wave 5, when 40% of men and 43% of women were dependent in at least one ADL. Similarly, 67% of men and 76% of women had difficulties with IADLs at Wave 1 and dependency changed little to 60% in men and 73% in women 9 years later at Wave 5. As noted by others (Gibson & Jackson, 1992), there were no differences between whites and blacks in difficulties with ADLs.

As found by others (Van Nostrand et al., 1993), the most common difficulties in ADLs were walking and bathing; the most common limitations in IADLs were housework and shopping. Although many respondents in our study required assistance with ADLs, they were living independently in the community. Whether these respondents received support from others for these activities was not measured but may account for their ability to remain in their own homes.

PSYCHOLOGICAL RESOURCES

Mastery represents a sense of control over events and reflects life circumstances. There is variability in the sense of control that individuals have. Some believe that they can do whatever they put their mind to and are responsible for their successes and failures. In contrast, others believe that they are not responsible for what happens to them and that their life circumstances are a matter of luck. Although elderly adults may underestimate their competencies in many areas (Bandura, 1981), declining physical competencies and increasing disability may present challenges that impede the ability of the very old to control their situations. Mastery or sense of control diminishes over time (Mirowsky, 1995), whereas the variability in mastery increases with age (Rodin, 1989).

Many of the stresses and situations that the very old face are chronic in nature (Krause & Jay, 1991), and control over their management or progression may not be possible. A strong sense of mastery and need to control a situation may not be effective in these situations, and using these strategies may lead to frustration or depression (Simons & West, 1985). Some have noted that a sense of low mastery may be associated with depressed mood (Pearlin, Menaghan, Lieberman, & Mullen, 1981), and others have found a significant positive association (Bienenfeld, Koenig, Larson, & Sherrill, 1997). However, this was not corroborated in our study. Here, two subscale scores for mastery were used instead of the total score because of the inherent two-factor structure in mastery found in the oldest-old (Roberts, Dunkle, & Haug, 1994b). Using these two subscales, greater depression was not significantly associated with greater global perceptions of control ($r = 0.10$) but was significantly related to control over events ($r = 0.34$, $p < 0.001$).

Some suggest that this decline in mastery with age may be related to the limitations associated with disease and disability (Mirowsky, 1995; Rodin, 1989). Using data from Wave 1, the relationship of mastery to ADLs and IADLs was assessed using the two factors of mastery. As global perceived control increased, independence significantly increased in ADL ($r = 0.24$, $p < 0.001$) and IADL ($r = 0.29$, $p < 0.001$). Similarly, these relationships were statistically significant for ratings of health ($r = 0.19$, $p < 0.001$) and ratings of how much health prevented doing things ($r = -0.28$, $p < 0.001$). That is, as perceptions of health declined and the more health interfered with activities, the global perception of control declined. In contrast, perceived control of events was significantly related only to ADL ($r = -0.24$), indicating that increasing dependence in ADLs was associated with lower control over events. Because these respondents were independent in almost all of their ADLs, ceiling effects and small variability in these activities may have precluded an accurate representation of the relationship between mastery and these activities.

Although physical disabilities were related to lower mastery, lower education has been found to decrease the effect of disability on the perceptions of control (Mirowsky, 1995). Moreover, education increases the sense of control (Busse & Maddox, 1985; Schaie, 1983). Findings from our study partially corroborate these findings. Using Wave 1 data, the two factors of mastery were used as the dependent variables and education, ADLs, and IADLs were used as the indepen-dent variables in multiple regression. ADLs, IADLs, and education explained 10.4% ($p < 0.0001$) of the variance in global perceived control, with only IADL having a statistically significant beta weight ($\beta = 0.25$, $p < 0.01$). Similarly, ADLs, IADLs, and education explained 3.6% of the variance in perceived control of events, with the beta weight for education approaching significance ($\beta = 0.19$, $p = 0.07$).

These findings may be explained by the problem-solving skills and successes experienced in addressing situations in life by those with more education. With greater education, individuals learn to solve more complex problems, and the problem-solving skills ac-quired increase their ability to successfully address other complex situations (Mirowsky, 1995). As individuals acquire more skills and successfully meet the challenges of life, their confidence in their ability to control events in their lives increases. Moreover, indepen-dence in IADLs may reflect the competence of the very old in per-forming daily activities. Perhaps, independence in these activities reinforces the abilities of the oldest-old to manage everyday activities and may reinforce their perceptions of control over situations in their lives.

Self-esteem is a reflection of the individual's evaluation of his or her self-worth and can be a resource in coping with the challenges of life (Rodin, 1989). In our study, self-esteem changed little from baseline interviews. Wave 5 survivors ($M = 11.3$) had significantly greater self-esteem at baseline than had Wave 4 survivors ($M = 10.7$). Similarly, at Wave 4, those completing the last interview ($M = 13.2$) had significantly greater self-esteem than Wave 4 survivors had ($M = 10.7$; $t [146] = 3.02$, $p < 0.001$). For Wave 5 survivors, self-esteem changed little by the last interview ($M = 13.3$).

Similarly, the proportion of respondents ranking feelings of worth as "extremely" or "a great deal" remained near 45% from baseline to Wave 4 for both those who survived to only Wave 4 and those who completed the entire 9 years of our study. By the end of our study, the proportion of respondents who similarly ranked their feelings of worth increased to 65%.

Because depression is associated with perceptions of low self-worth, it is not surprising that lower self-esteem was significantly related to greater depression ($r = -0.23$) at the baseline interview. Whether self-esteem changes as life circumstances change or the individual becomes more dependent and unable to control events is not known.

SOCIAL RESOURCES

Social support embodies social resources and is the interaction between people. Social support has most frequently been conceptualized as the provision of tangible support, although emotional and informational support have also been identified. In community-dwelling elders, men and women mobilized social support differently in response to stress as related to impaired mobility and difficulty in the performance of ADL and household IADLs (Roberts, Anthony, Matejczyk, & Moore, 1994). Women with greater mobility had greater tangible support and, to a lesser extent, greater emotional support, whereas men used very little tangible and emotional support in this circumstance.

Not all-social support is associated with positive outcomes. Negative social interchanges may be more difficult for elderly adults who often are dealing with chronic stressors (Rook, 1994). Negative social interchanges have been associated with greater depression, which exacerbates the negative effects of stress (Stephens et al., 1987; Rook, 1994); positive exchanges have not been significantly related to this outcome (Finch & Zautra, 1992). In a study with older adults, others found that negative interactions increased negative aspects of psychological well-being, and positive interaction increased the positive aspects of well-being (Ingersoll-Dayton, Morgan, & Antonucci, 1997).

As individuals age, disease and disability become more prevalent while the social network diminishes in size and composition. These changes may alter the interactions with the social network and the demands made on persons who have the potential to provide support. What once may have been an adequate social network may no longer be so because the needs for care and assistance grow with the prevalence of chronic and acute disease and disability. These changes may place the oldest-old at greater risk for institutionalization and further decline in physical and mental health. In spite of the extensive social support research, little is known about the social network and interactions among the very old.

Composition of the Social Network

To be a resource, there must be contacts with members of the social network and help must be available in times of need (Fillenbaum, 1988). The size of the social network, that is, the people available for social support, reflects the potential of support. In our study, the availability of support to provide care did not significantly change from baseline to 9 years later ($M = 4.0$ and 4.1, respectively).

Composition of the social network is reflected by marital status, friends, family, and confidants. In the convoy theory of social support, the social network comprises concentric circles around an individual (Antonucci, 1986; Kahn & Antonucci, 1980). The innermost circle contains the most intimate, and subsequent circles are more distant relationships.

Spouses compose an inner circle and are likely to provide the most support. Although in our study 52.2% of men were married, only 11% of women were married, which is a smaller proportion for persons 75 and older than reported in the 1997 *Statistical Abstract of the United States* (Bureau of the Census). Respondents who were divorced or single (8.8%, $n = 17$) were all women. Clearly, women lose a major source of social support. These very old respondents had little spousal support, with only 21% of subjects ($n = 40$) married at Wave 1. This proportion is similar to that found among octogenarians (Bould et al., 1988; Martin, Poon, Kim, & Johnson, 1996) but significantly more than the 10% found by others (Rosenwaike, 1985). Rosenwaike (1985) studied the same cohort at least 10 years earlier than our study. Thus, the respondents in his study may represent a cohort whose life expectancy was lower than the cohort in our study, and significantly more may have survived into their 80s in our study than those in Rosenwaike's study (1985). Although many respondents in our study were married at the baseline interview, none were married 9 years later, when 88% of the respondents were widowed. Clearly, many of the survivors now in their 90s had lost a significant person in their social support network.

The inner circle of social support more likely comprises persons living in the same household as the older adult. This proximity facilitates frequent and often intimate interactions, and individuals in the same household may provide a significant amount of social support. However, at the first interview, nearly 62% lived alone, a proportion significantly greater than the 41% in those over 75 years (Bureau of the Census, 1997), the 38% among those 85 and older (Bould et al., 1988), and the 47% among octogenarians (Martin et al., 1996). A greater proportion of respondents may live alone because they are healthier and less disabled than those represented in the U.S. Census or other studies (Bould et al., 1988; Martin et al., 1996). It was not possible to assess whether this explains the differences in those living alone in our study.

Nearly 14% of the respondents in our study lived with a child, 3% lived with a grandchild, and 5% lived with others. This household composition was similar to octogenarians: 8% lived with a child, 8% with a grandchild, 2% with others (Martin et al., 1996). In contrast, only one Wave 5 survivor lived alone. Most were living with non–family members; one was living with a child, another with a paid helper, and another with an unspecified relative.

The next concentric circle of social support comprises family and friends. Two thirds or more of the respondents had living children, with more than 88% of them living in the Cleveland area. Approximately, 40% of Wave 4 and 5 survivors had living siblings; at Wave 5, only 14% had a living sibling. Nearly 96% had a confidant at baseline, but only 73% had one 9 years later.

Similar to other longitudinal studies that included very old subjects (Field & Minkler, 1989; van Tilburg, 1998), the social network of respondents in our study did decline over time. Although many women were without spousal support, they did have confidants, family, and friends in their second tier of their social network who could be available to provide social support. These findings provide support for the deficit model of social support in which support is hypothesized to decline with advancing age (Baltes & Carstensen, 1996).

Data regarding specific individuals in the social network and those who could provide assistance when needed depict a picture that further supports the deficit model of social support (Baltes & Carstensen, 1996). As noted earlier, the availability of persons to provide help when needed is crucial to effective social support (Fillenbaum,

1998). These very old respondents most frequently identified a child as someone who could provide occasional assistance if needed (25% at baseline to 42% at Wave 4 for those interviewed at all four time points). Although 78.3% had living children at the last interview at Wave 5, only 21.7% identified a child as being able to provide assistance. These children may have been in their 60s and 70s and may have had chronic conditions and disabilities that prevented them from providing support to their very old parents. Alternately, many children may have moved too far away to provide assistance. Although 40% had living siblings, none were identified as being able to provide even occasional help. These siblings may have been too disabled to provide support or lived too far to offer it. However, 30.4% identified a friend as providing the most support, whereas 13% had a neighbor who provided the most support. These findings suggest that the inner circle of intimate spouse and family members was greatly reduced or absent and that the second circle of the social network provided more assistance than did spouses or family members.

Other evidence suggests that the size of the social network decreased with age. At Wave 1, less than 5% of the respondents knew no one to visit, and this increased to nearly 10% at Wave 4 and 17% at Wave 5. Approximately 70% of respondents knew five or more people to visit at the first interview, but this proportion dropped to 60% at Waves 4 and 5.

These findings support the assertion of others (Baltes & Carstensen, 1996; Bould et al., 1988) that the size of the social network shrinks with age. However, these findings may also be explained by increasing isolation from family and friends because of poor health of these individuals (van Tilburg, 1998) or needs for assistance by others in the social network (Baltes & Carstensen, 1996). Moreover, the diminished size of the social network is a critical problem in the very old who, because of impairments in hearing, vision, and mobility, may not be able to easily access individuals in their social network at a time when they may need them the most.

Frequency of Social Contacts

The older adult may identify persons as being part of their social network and yet have very little contact with these people. For example, friends or family members may be unable to interact because of disability or illness, and they may be too distant geographically for easy interaction. An older adult with a small network who interacts frequently may receive significantly more social support than would a person with a larger network but few interactions with it. Hence, the frequency of contact may be a better indicator of social interaction required for social support. In our study, the frequency of social interactions did not significantly change from baseline to 9 years later.

Although nearly 60% had daily phone contact with people, slightly more than half visited with others two to six times a week. Approximately two thirds of the respondents maintained weekly contact with their siblings. Of those alive at the last interview, 57% had daily visits. At the first interview, approximately 17% did not have visits from anyone in a month, and this proportion declined to 9% for the survivors at Wave 5, which may reflect the increase in the proportion receiving daily visits (17%, 21%, and 39%, for Waves 1, 4, and 5, respectively).

Many respondents said they would have liked more frequent contact with family and friends. Although those who survived to the last interview were happy with the contact (74%, 82%, and 52% for Waves 1, 4, and 5, respectively), smaller proportions of the Wave 4 survivors were satisfied with the frequency of interactions (55% at baseline and 41% 18 months later). Although these changes over time may reflect a decrease in the size of the social network, they may also be accounted for by isolation from friends and family because of poor health (van Tilburg, 1998). This hypothesis is partially supported by the finding that 68% of the respondents in our study were lonely—findings significantly different than in the Georgia Centenarian Study in which less than 10% were lonely (Martin et al., 1996).

In summary, little change in the life circumstances of these very old respondents was found over the 9-year study. Although the oldest-old in the present sample had several chronic conditions, their use of health-care resources remained low. In spite of chronic illness and dependencies in at least one ADL or IADL, respondents were still able to live independently in the community. Whether their social networks and social support received by the respondents allowed them to continue living in their own homes is unknown because the formal and informal social supports necessary for this were not studied. The findings from our study can only be generalized to the very old living in an urban area and in their own homes.

Interestingly, those who completed the last interview of this 9-year longitudinal study were significantly healthier and less dependent at baseline and 18 months later than were those who only survived to Wave 4. Whether the Wave 5 survivors were healthier their entire lives and engaged in more health-promoting behaviors is unknown, but these differences may have influenced their survival during the entire 9 years of our study. Perhaps the Wave 4 survivors had already experienced a decline in health and independence, whereas those who lived to Wave 5 may have just begun to experience such a decline. However, those respondents alive for the last interview 9 years from baseline did experience significant decline in their health, independence, and social network from Wave 4. More prospective studies with larger sample sizes are needed to elucidate the trajectory of change among older adults into their 80s and older.

CHAPTER 3

Self-Perception Over Time

S elf-perception has been a well-investigated topic across the life span but not among the very old. Many things influence self-perception, for example, age, gender, and physical capacity. With young children, the very recognition of the self develops over time (Sugarman, 1987). Teenagers are frequently depicted as self-centered, absorbed in their "self." Self-perception among the old is often affected by negative stereotypes of being old (Atchley, 1999), as well as by the physical changes that come with age. Women have been described as becoming more assertive with age whereas men become less so (Thurnher, 1979). Gender stereotypes are substantially represented, with 34% of self-concept items in gerontological studies concerning perception of self (Lowenthal et al., 1975). Although it is recognized that many aspects of life affect self-perception, how the self changes with age is unclear (George & Binstock, 1990). What work exists on self-perception over the life span compares younger people with older ones. There is no knowledge on how self-perception changes for older people as they age and face the physical and social changes that accompany growing older. Because the subjects in this study are over the age of 85, we discuss self-perception among these very old people, as they grow older.

BACKGROUND

There is agreement that humans strive to create stable and positive self-images and that they seem to perceive information selectively in order to achieve this goal (Breytspraak, 1984). Rosenberg (1979) found that people continue to view themselves consistently, holding the same self-view that they developed earlier in their lives. This seems to persist even when these perceptions did not appear to be valid objectively. This consistency has the positive effect of providing direction to one's life and predictability for social interaction; in other words, people have the opportunity to predict another's behavior from one social situation to another. Atchley (1982) also supported consistency but believed that fewer roles may mean less conflict, not a self that is inconsistent with the past. Thus, he supported greater consistency with age, believing that older people work at maintaining their self-perception.

Others argue that pressures toward consistency lessen with age because people have fewer roles they need to fill (role theory) and because they begin to shed the concern and attachment to demands of everyday life (disengagement theory). Rosow (1985) believes this is due to the fact that older people's behavior is of less consequence because they have fewer "normative expectations" for their behavior.

SENSE OF SELF ACROSS THE LIFE SPAN

How is a consistent sense of self maintained across the life span when so many changes (e.g., health, relationships, appearance, etc.) occur with increasing age (Gergen, 1991)? There are multiple sources of self-knowledge. One source occurs through self-attribution, in which the individual determines the cause of his or her behavior in an effort to make sense of things that happen. Second, there is reflected appraisal in which one sees oneself through other's opinions (Cooley, 1902). Another source is information generated by comparing oneself with others (Suls & Miller, 1977). Last, through the process of identification, the elder has role models, and attempts are made to emulate them.

SELF-ATTRIBUTION

Heider (1958) suggests that people tend to search for causation in order to make their world more predictable. Causality can be attributed to either personal or environmental characteristics, with personal attribution being more likely to result in a poorer self-image. Cooper and Goethals (1981) suggest that because old people face so much change, they are constantly in the position of looking for appropriate attributions for their behaviors. In ambiguous cases, the attribution is often to internal factors, such as biological aging. This can be particularly deleterious to the self-concept of someone who then feels that there is nothing that can mitigate the circumstance. In order to protect one's self-perception, it is important to see failures and negative circumstances as a result of external forces.

SELF AS A PRODUCT OF SOCIAL INTERACTION

Self is the product of social interaction as explicated through symbolic interaction theory. The person perceives what others think of him or her. This information, though, does not necessarily correspond to the person's self-concept because of the active tendency to make self look better (Shrauger & Schoeneman, 1979). It is not the simple absorption of others' appraisals, but the active involvement of the individual in influencing the information presented to others that affects the appraisal (Goffman, 1959).

Are older people more or less affected by these appraisals than are younger people? Cooper and Goethals (1981) suggest that they are more sensitive because of the loss of many friends and family through death. Without a cohesive reference group, they may be more susceptible to the negative stereotypes of being old.

SELF AS A RESULT OF COMPARISON WITH OTHERS

People also evaluate themselves by comparing themselves to others. Reference group theory (Festinger, 1954) suggests that people compare themselves with others of similar ability or characteristics. More recent research (Cooper & Goethals, 1981) shows that the comparison is typically downward to those doing worse. This is referred to as a "defensive comparison" (Cooper & Goethals, 1981), when people assume that they will not perform as well and try to improve their self-image by noting that there are others who would do worse. Festinger (1954) and Albert (1977) suggest that people also make temporal comparisons against themselves. For example, the older person may think of how they were earlier in life as compared with later in life. Life review is an example of this, in which older persons view their lives as a whole with greater likelihood of experiencing consistency in past and present self-concepts (Lewis, 1971).

Suls and Mullen (1982) note that the comparison process seems to change across the life span. At certain points, comparison is made with those who are similar such as in adolescence and mid to late adulthood, comparisons are made with those who are dissimilar. Upward and downward comparison occurs in order to convince oneself that one is better off (Taylor, 1989). Others find that social comparison is less likely to be of benefit to elders because of their reduced need to have socially desirable behavior (Hansson, 1986; Hansson, Hogan, & Jones, 1984).

Identification

Identification is related to social comparison because it is likely that people will compare themselves to those slightly ahead of them in some manner. Goals are set and people are chosen as models. Lowenthal et al. (1975) notes that this future orientation for older people may be difficult to maintain in the face of growing infirmities. Finding role models can also be a problem in that the older person may not have wide contact with other elders. This is a particular problem among the very old because of fewer members of this age group.

Whereas much of the work on self-perception has been influenced by the social theories mentioned earlier, there are those who are interested in the topic from a more psychological perspective. Labou-vie-Vief, Chiodo, Goguen, and Diehl (1995) have promoted a life span cognitive perspective. To date, much of the work in this area has been with children (Cross & Markus, 1991). Developmentally, there is a movement from concrete conceptual characteristics in childhood to more complex and abstract conceptualization characteristics, such as ideals and intentions developing in adulthood (Case, 1991; Fischer, Shaver, & Carnochan, 1990). Labouvie-Vief et al. (1995) state, "The self and others and their interrelationships are framed in relatively organized, codified, and abstract expectations" (p. 405). In comparing adolescents, middle-aged people, and those who are older, these authors found that the complexity of self-representations peaked in midlife. Preadolescents and older people appeared to have the lowest level of self-representations, describing themselves using conventional traits and characteristics. One 94-year-old woman in our study demonstrated this category when she described herself as saying, "I come from a family of 10—if my mother wouldn't have had miscarriages we would have been 15. My brothers were captains in the navy in Britain. I've been here 65 years." Another woman, age 89, said, "I have snow-white hair. I weigh 135 pounds. Just an ordinary person."

In summary, it appears that the self develops and responds to the social context in which the person lives. It also acts as a filter through which the social structure is experienced. As George and Binstock (1990) concluded after reviewing the literature on self-perception, "Older people retain a sense of self that is comfortable and positive" (p. 199). Bengtson et al. (1986) suggest that changes in self-perception stem from changes in social situations and not developmental issues. Filipp and Klauer (1986) support the notion of consistency by suggesting that self-concept is "protected and preserved" in the adult life span. Labouvie-Vief et al. (1995), examining the self-concept from a cognitive perspective, suggest that self-concept may be related to development.

RELEVANCE TO THE VERY OLD

Although research on self-perception has included older people, there is no work that examines this concept among the very old. This age group is particularly interesting to examine because people who are very old are more likely to experience many role changes with the death of friends and family (Field & Minkler, 1988). In addition, most people over the age of 85 experience compromised functional abilities and declining health, which can have dramatic effects on self-perception (Atchley, 1999).

In an effort to better understand the self-perception of very old people, we interviewed a sample of those 85 years of age and older over a 9-year span.

MEASURES FOR THE ANALYSES

Self-Perception

The measure of self-perception was an open-ended response to the question, "Could you tell me in general how you feel about being your age?" This measure was embedded in a semi-structured interview. Two researchers coded the responses separately. Each initially read through all responses from all five waves of data and devised a list of categories. Before coding the responses, the researchers agreed on the categories to be used. Coding discrepancies were then reconciled between the two. If respondents identified more than one feeling about being their age, only the initial feeling was coded and included in the analysis. Interrater reliability was 0.85. This self-description question had an interrater reliability of 0.75.

The remaining measures described here are included for correlational purposes in order to gain a better understanding of what factors are related to the self-concept of the very old. Further description of the variables can be found in the Appendix.

Key Findings

How do subjects feel about being their age? Table 3.1 identifies the range of codes generated from Waves 1 and 5 of data for the open-ended question, "Could you tell me in general how you feel about being your age?" Clearly the range of responses is large, with some seeing their age as an opportunity, others having no concerns about their age, and still others focusing on physical and social losses.

TABLE 3.1 Codes for Feeling Age

Age not a concern
Disbelief about age
Social loss
Potential social loss
Physical or functional loss
Potential for physical or functional loss
Dependence
Opportunity
Regret
Glad to be healthy
Social fulfillment
Concerns related to death
Orientation toward future
Orientation toward past
Orientation toward present
Positive feelings
Negative feelings
Fortunate
Independent
Nothing
Accepting
Ability to do things
Want life over
Pain, discomfort
Lack of responsibility
Basic function
Adjusting
Do not feel age
Other

Comparing Respondents in Their 80s with Those in Their 90s

Also meaningful is the frequency of responses concerning the various ways these very old people feel about being their age as it increases. Table 3.2 deals with responses at Wave 1 of the panel of subjects surviving at least through Time 4 ($n = 153$). The respondents were divided into two groups: those who were under the age of 90 and those who were 90 and over. With functional decline increasing with age, it was hypothesized that function would be worse in those in their 90 as compared with those in their 80s and would potentially

TABLE 3.2   Distribution of Responses by Age (Wave 1; $n = 153$)*

Feeling	Age: 80s		Age: 90s	
	n	%	n	%
Age not a concern	19	17	9	23
Positive feelings	31	27	15	38
Disbelief about age	8	7	3	
Social loss	5	4		
Physical or functional loss	8	7	3	8
Regret	2	2		
Glad to be healthy	6	5	2	
Social fulfillment	2	2		
Orientation to past			1	3
Negative feelings	8	7		
Fortunate	9	8	3	8
Independent	1	1	1	3
Accepting	6	5		
Do not feel age	8	7	3	8
Totals	$n = 113$	100	$n = 40$	100

*Cross-sectional data
[†]No significant differences between two age groups in self-reported health, ADL, IADL, and mastery.

influence how these respondents felt about their age. Further, it provided an opportunity to compare groups among the very old, a view rarely taken in gerontological research (Martin, Poon, Kim, & Johnson, 1996).

When considering those subjects in their 80s, the range of responses used was much greater than for those in their 90s. Responses that occurred in the younger group but not the older included feelings of social loss, regret, negative feelings, and acceptance. There was only one category of response that appeared among the older group but not the younger (orientation toward the past). The most common responses in each group were the same: age was not a concern and having positive feelings toward being their age.

For those who felt that age was not a concern, one respondent said, "Doesn't bother me. I'm just going on living. I go on one day at a time. I'm going on with my work, my housework, that is, and I'm really just taking things as they come." Another said, "Well frankly, I don't give it much thought. I just enjoy being alive." The second most frequently mentioned feeling was of a positive nature. One respondent said, "I feel good. I feel better than most people my age. I don't have any regrets in my life. I've had a good life. I've been around the world. I've been my own boss—built two plants. I've had a good life." Another said, "I feel fine. I wash my hair and see I didn't have time to oil and set it. When I go out of here to church, they don't believe I'm almost 100."

Although there were no statistically significant differences among major physical measures of self-rated health, ADLs, and self-esteem and in the two mastery factors between these two age groups (those in their 80s and those in their 90s) at Wave 1, it should be recalled that the 154 subjects were selected in a convenience sample where they were residing in the community. Therefore, it is very likely that the lack of variability by age group at Time 1 is due to sample selection. This lack of difference in ADL functioning among people in their 80s and those in their 90s was also found in another cross-sectional analysis of residents living in the community (Bondevik & Skogstad, 1995). The findings, based on asking them how they felt about their age, indicated that those in their 80s perceived themselves differently than did those in their 90s.

Change in Self-Perception

Based on panel data over the five waves, the responses from the 23 subjects who were interviewed at Wave 1 and then 9 years later at Wave 5 revealed what changes had occurred in physical and psychological functioning that could contribute to feelings about being their age. Using analysis of variance data, the 23 subjects who were interviewed at Wave 5 (1995), when they were in their 90s were compared with data from this same group of subjects at Wave 1 (1986), when they were in their 80s. Results indicate that significant differences occurred when these subjects reached their 90s. These subjects had worse instrumental and physical functioning in ADLs and a poorer sense of mastery. There were no significant differences in self-esteem or self-rated health (see chapter 2 for a summary).

Data on these 23 subjects at Wave 1 were also compared with data on themselves 9 years later at Wave 5 using repeated measures

(Manova). There were also statistically significant differences. Although at Wave 5 these subjects ($n = 23$) rated their overall health, physical and instrumental functioning, and mastery lower than they did at Wave 1, there was no statistically significant difference between their self-esteem scores at Waves 1 and 5.

This same comparison of these subjects who were in their 80s at Wave 1 and in their 90s at Wave 5 was made concerning their feelings about their age. These findings were similar to Wave 1 (Table 3.3) in the range of responses. The most frequent response was potential for physical or functional loss at Wave 1 and positive feelings at Wave 5. This is understandable, with significant functional decline between Waves 1 and 5. There is a notable difference between Waves 1 and 5, in that no one over the age of 90 at Wave 5 mentioned social or physical loss, the potential for physical or functional loss, or concerns related to death. Although subjects at Wave 5 were significantly different in their physical and psychological functional abilities than they were at Wave 1 (9 years earlier), these aspects of aging were not what they chose to identify when talking with the interviewer.

TABLE 3.3   Longitudinal Data (Waves 1 and 5; $n = 23$)

Feeling	Wave 1 (80s)		Wave 5 (90s)	
	n	%	n	%
Age not concern	7	30		
Disbelief about age			4	17
Social loss	1	4	1	4
Physical or function loss	2	9		
Potential physical or functional loss	13	57		
Concerns related to death	1	4		
Orientation toward future				
Positive feelings	2	9	9	39
Glad to be healthy	1	4		
Negative feelings	2	9	3	13
Fortunate	4	17	1	4
Adjusting			2	9
Nothing			2	9
Want life over			1	4
Totals	$n = 23$	100	$n = 23$	100

They more frequently talked of positive feelings (39%) and disbelief about their age (17%). There were 13% who mentioned negative feelings about their age. One person said, "I don't like it." Another said, "Sometimes I become disgusted with it. It takes so much more time to do things." In general, though, these comments were not specifically related to a particular aspect of life.

In examining the responses in the two most common categories (age is not a concern and positive feelings), we find many responses in which the elders compare their lives to others who are worse off. One respondent in her 80s said, "Well, I really never think about it to tell you the truth. If a person is well, it really doesn't matter. I think I can do more than most of my friends my age." Another woman in her 90s said, "I feel good; as long as I feel good and eat good, then I'm okay. My life has been better when I compare it to my girlfriend."

When examining those with positive feelings about their age, the same comparison is found. One woman in her 80s said, "I feel good. I like it. I can't go back. I feel good because a lot of people my age are gone already." Another says, "I don't feel that old. I see my friends who are crippled with arthritis and bedridden and so I don't feel that old really."

Many of these comparisons were of a direct nature. People mentioned someone they knew or had seen that functioned more poorly. One woman said: "I don't think of it at all. I don't feel like some of my older relatives—they were all wrinkled up and stooped and I'm not." Numerous examples were found of elders comparing themselves to others who were in worse condition; other forms of comparison also emerged, such as comparing themselves to themselves at an earlier time. They noted that their condition was worse or, in many more cases, the same as 20 or more years earlier or that it had improved with time. One woman said, "I can't believe I'm my age because I feel as though I'm 30 years old. I have no health problems." Another said, "I don't believe I'm 90. Many times I sit around and think am I really this old? I do everything the same as I did 20 years ago. God's been good to me. I take pride with my family, 24 grandchildren, and 36 great grandchildren." They also drew a parallel with younger people, who were in good condition, when they were in good condition as well.

Comparison was also of a more implicit nature. Statements were made that implied that things could be worse, that they had things for which to be grateful, or that they felt fortunate, such as "You know there is a saying, don't regret getting old. It's a privilege denied to many." One said, "In general, I don't regret growing old. People 62 or 45 fall over and that is it, they're gone." Another said, "I'm just glad I am 89. I've lived longer than others, and I feel I have a good life."

Lastly, the longitudinal data allowed comparison over time of how the 23 subjects felt about their age when they were in their 80s and then 9 years later when they were in their 90s (Wave 5), with particular attention paid to how these feelings related to their level of ADL functioning. Is how very old people feel about their age related to their health? The physical functioning of the respondents between Waves 1 and 5 were compared. In 43% of the cases ($n = 9$), the functional ability remained the same (one person improved) over the 9-year study period (Table 3.4). Among these 9 cases, 1 person's feelings about age became more negative. In the other 13 cases, in which functional ability declined among all, only 4 people's feelings about their age became more negative. Six of the 13 subjects, however, had a decline in functional ability of a greater magnitude (3–8 points). Two of these 6 people's feelings about their age changed from negative to positive over the 9 years, 1 remained negative, 1 remained positive at both time points, and 1 who had felt positively about her age at Wave 1 felt negatively at Wave 5. Unfortunately, there were no data available to determine when in the 9-year period the functional decline occurred. The amount of time that had elapsed since the loss of functional ability obviously could have a bearing on quality of life and be related to the degree of adjustment made to the ability level.

Examinations of individual profiles showed that 5 of 8 subjects whose feelings about their age improved over the 9-year period actually had lower functional ability at Wave 5 than they did at Wave 1. Among 5 subjects who felt more negative about their age, 3 had lower functioning ability. However, 9 subjects whose feelings about their age were consistently positive across the two waves experienced a decline in function. In fact, 4 had lower functional ability and 1 subject who was consistently negative had a lower functional score

TABLE 3.4   Longitudinal Data (*n* = 23)

Feelings of Self	Case #	Wave 1 (80s)	Wave 5 (90s)
Negative to positive feelings	1	Physical or functional loss	Adjusting
	2	Potential physical or functional loss	Positive feeling
	3	Negative feelings	Age not concern
	4	Physical or functional loss	Positive feeling
	5	Concerns related to death	Age not concern
	6*	Social loss	Positive feelings
	7*	Potential for physical of functional loss	Fortunate
Positive to negative feeling	8	Fortunate	Negative feeling
	9*	Glad to be healthy	Negative feeling
	10	Age not a concern	Nothing good
	11	Fortunate	Want life over
	12	Fortunate	Negative feelings
Consistently positive	13	Age not a concern	Age not concern
	14	Positive feeling	Positive feeling
	15	Age not concern	Positive feelings
	16	Age not concern	Age not concern
	17*	Age not concern	Positive feelings
	18	Age not concern	Positive feelings
	19	Fortunate	Positive feelings
	20*	Age not concern	Disbelief about age
	21	Positive feeling	Positive feeling
Consistently negative	22*	Negative feelings	Nothing
	23	Potential for physical or social loss	Nothing

*where decline in ADL was at least 3 points between Waves 1 and 5

at Wave 5 than at Wave 1. These comparisons indicate that in a significant number of cases, even as these very old people experience a decline in function, their view of age remains positive.

DISCUSSION

The purpose of this chapter was to examine the self-perception among the very old as perceived through their self-description of feelings about being their age. Comparing people in their 80s with those in their 90s allowed for greater insight into how they felt about their age as they grew older, when there was a greater likelihood of experiencing functional decline. In the face of such decline, a potential influence on self-perception, these very old subjects were prime candidates for examining how they felt about their age. Findings indicate that even when experiencing functional decline, many of these very old people felt positively about their age. This is particularly true among those over 90 years of age who use comparison as a means of evaluating themselves.

Initially, those in the Wave 1 sample who had completed Wave 4 as well ($n = 154$) who were in their 80s were contrasted with those in their 90s. Anticipating greater functional limitations in those age 90+, there were no significant functional differences between these two age groups at Wave 1, perhaps due to the fact they were originally chosen in a convenience sample that resided in the community. Nevertheless, people in these two groups noted different things when asked how they felt about being their age. Those under the age of 90 mentioned issues of social loss, regret, negative feelings, and acceptance. But people over 90 years of age were less likely to focus on aspects of loss. Although loss certainly was a part of their human experience, especially for people over age 90, there were more frequent expressions of how rare it was to live into their 90s and how fortunate they felt.

People in their 80s and 90s compare their lives to others, a technique used to help them feel more positive about their age. Johnson and Barer (1997) also found that their very old respondents de-emphasized health problems by using positive comparisons. There is evidence that perception is a strong force in how older people evaluate their health. Kuetner (1992) found that some old people are health optimists " . . . having more favorable health perceptions than their levels of physical functioning objectively allow" (p. 534). Social comparison theory offers an explanation of quality of life in old age that sheds light on how this optimism may be maintained. Taylor (1983) found that individuals use very selective criteria when comparing themselves with others in order to be convinced that they are better off. The comparison in old age seems to be more likely with others who are dissimilar (Suls & Mullen, 1982), so those who are very old with severe or chronic illness, or both, selectively compare themselves with others in their age group who are in worse shape (i.e., more functionally limited or dead). The comparison continues over time as the person's health changes, always seeking a perception that enhances control and predictability, thus allowing for more effective coping (Filipp & Klauer, 1986).

These respondents describe how they use age peers as a reference point to describe their own health as better. In this study, the comparison was not always with others who are dissimilar, as suggested by Suls and Mullen (1982). In many cases, the comparison was to those in good shape with whom the person felt similarity. In general, these people believe that they are rare, that it is unusual and special that they have lived so long. This view is supported by work by Johnson and Barer (1997), who also found that people over age 85 referred to their special status as survivors, as individuals who had outlived others their age. That fact in and of itself was a central feature in their description of how they felt about their age. They found ways to feel fortunate without focusing on loss, which is more universal as people grew older from their 80s to their 90s.

CONCLUSION

The results of these analyses indicate that self-perception is influenced by individuals' subjective interpretation of how they feel about being their age, which was based on information gathered by their use of social comparison. As long as they saw themselves as functioning better than others, their quality of life was more positive, regardless of the objective reality of their functional ability as measured by conventional functional ability scales. Carlson, Berg, and Wenestan (1991) support these findings on the value of the influence of the individual's subjective interpretation of life. The work in this chapter extends understanding of the subjective interpretation by identifying social comparison as the mechanism promoting a more positive sense of self-image among the very old.

CHAPTER 4

The Future of the Oldest Old

H aving goals may be an important component of successful aging, providing a frame of reference that older adults use to evaluate their lives (Rapkin & Fischer, 1992). Emmons and Diener (1986) found that positive affect was related to the existence and attainment of goals whereas negative affect was related to lack of goal attainment. The "capacity to anticipate" influences mental health, happiness (Diener, 1984), and psychological well-being (Holahan, 1988) as well as promotes successful aging (Kastenbaum, 1982).

The thought that very old people think much about the future seems anomalous to some people. Marcus and Herzog (1991) believe that old age is a "period of disengagement from thinking about the future and a time of casting off possible selves." This could be the case among the oldest-old, who are more likely to experience poor health and greater hassles and be closer to death. In this vein, Nuttin (1984) suggests that having no goals (having no future time perspective) may better serve older people who face adversity or unforeseeable circumstances that may strongly affect predictability of the future. For some people, having goals may not promote successful aging; it may even foster mental health problems.

To date, there is no information on the relationship of goals to the mental health of people who are very old. This chapter explores the goals of very old people as well as the relationship between their goals and their mental health.

FUTURE TIME PERSPECTIVE

Throughout life, many people have a notion of their future. They may have plans for the afternoon or for things that they want to accomplish in coming decades. As such, they set goals; they have a future time perspective.

Where do these goals come from? The future cannot be segregated from the past or present. According to Whitehead, "what we perceive as present is a vivid fringe of memory tinged with anticipation . . . the past and the future meet and mingle in the ill-defined present. . . . The future does not simply exist, it is constructed by us and perceived as a series of expected presents" (Burton, 1976, p. 35). Our conception of the future is the antecedent of it and it resides in the present (Hendricks, 1982). Many different motivational forces that combine achievement, maintenance, and disengagement influence goals and support related themes (Rapkin & Fischer, 1992), suggesting that elders want different things out of life. Therefore, goals vary (Rapkin & Fischer, 1992) and may be important to successful adjustment in older age.

The goals for which older people strive include maintenance of the status quo in areas of health and autonomy, independence, capacity for self-care, and social contacts and aspirations pertaining to the well-being of family members (Lapierre, Bouffard, & Bastin, 1992–1993). It is not clear, however whether these goals, culled from a group of old respondents, are reflective of goals for the very old.

The work that exists on the topic of goals for the very old age group is limited. In exploring time orientation in their study of the very old, Johnson and Barer (1993) found a tendency toward present orientation but did not examine goal orientation. A more recent study using a sample of German elders (Mayer et al., 1999) reported that most older people still have life goals described as hopes and fears or as activities and interests. Very old age is characterized by a future orientation that covers a broad range of goals, with the most prominent hopes and fears involving personal characteristics and health. Goals of self-acceptance, autonomy, and positive relations with others were most prevalent (Mayer et al., 1999). Substantial individual variation had been noted, but there were few age/cohort differences (Smith & Baltes, 1999).

Earlier researchers working on the topic of future time perspective in the 1960s and 1970s explored the reason why older people think of their future. At some point in later adulthood a confrontation with time occurs (Rakowski, 1979). This confrontation is the result of a "personal realization of mortality," with the individual's perspective shifting from time lived to time to live before death (Carstensen, 1999). Whether this focus on time until death includes identifying goals has been explored for middle-aged people, as well as among those in later life (Hooker & Siegler, 1993; Lapierre et al., 1992–1993).

This realization of mortality may result in a shift in personal expectations regarding the possible achievement of goals and thus restrict the person's personal projection into the future (Carstensen & Freund, 1994; Costa & Kastenbaum, 1967; Kastenbaum, 1963; Rakowski, 1979). At some point these older people could be at risk for developing a time perspective that limits their perceived future through not setting goals (losing control), thus resulting in mental health problems such as depression. Limiting one's perspective could be viewed as limiting one's sense of control, a concept that has a negative effect on mental health (Rodin, 1986). On the other hand, as stated earlier, having no goals may actually be helpful to those facing adversity (Nuttin, 1984), in that limiting one's sense of control through curtailing goal setting could enhance perceived control and result in better mental health, for example, less depression. To date, the role of goals in the mental health of the very old has not been explored.

PERCEIVED CONTROL

Perceived control is the belief that a person can obtain desired outcomes (Skinner et al., 1988). Positive outcomes, such as better mental health, result from perceived control (Thompson, 1981). Unfortunately, unlike younger adults who frequently experience increasing social, financial, and functional competence as they age, older adults typically experience a variety of major life changes.

Older adults face changes in personal factors associated with aging that affect all who live long enough to experience them, possibly diminishing opportunities for control with advancing age (Rodin & Timko, 1992) or the older person's capacity to perceive control (Holahan & Holahan, 1987).

Rodin (1986) suggested that having less control has a negative affect on mental health and that this relationship increases with age. Being able to respond to these age-related changes and incorporate them into purposeful, self-determined activities such as goals can lead to a sense of control and subsequent adaptation (i.e., less depression and a greater sense of well-being) (Baltes & Baltes, 1986). The connection of personal goals and control can provide meaning to life (Brandtstadter & Rothermund, 1994; Brandtstadter & Baltes-Gotz, 1990).

In more recent work, researchers attempted to understand control in the face of adversity. People usually begin by using direct (instrumental) means to cope. Other efforts of control such as disengagement from goals, adjustment of standards, and self-enhancing comparisons are used if instrumental means are not unsuccessful (Carstensen & Freund, 1994). Schulz, Heckhausen, and Locher (1991) found that when people confronted uncontrollable events, they modified attribution of responsibility in some instances. Sometimes cognitive adaptations such as decreasing the desirability of the goal or the favorable social comparison occurred if the person was unable to directly change the circumstance (Heckhausen & Schultz, 1991). In addition, an immunization process in which information is processed in a way that reduces negative feedback about the self could be at work (Brandtstadter & Greve, 1994).

In a similar vein, Baltes and Baltes (1990) viewed adaptation to aging as an older person's narrowing of focus. They called this selective optimization with compensation (SOC). When loss occurs people select the most important goals and try to sustain related activities, discarding less-important goals. This selection of alternative behaviors aids in minimizing failure so that a sense of mastery and control can be maintained.

This change could result in a change in goal salience (Carstensen & Freund, 1994) as an older person faces threats (Brandtstadter & Greve, 1994) and opportunities (Carstensen & Freund, 1994). This may be particularly true among the very old, those persons over the age of 85. Possibly, certain goals are more prominent at specific times in the life span. Social goals may change over time, with younger people having future-oriented, long-term goals that change to present focused, emotional, related goals later on in life (Carstensen & Freund, 1994).

The revision of goals may be based on the individual's seeking a level of "just manageable difficulty" (Carstensen & Freund, 1994, p. 139). The person feels challenged given their existing resources and competencies. A change in capacities often necessitates a change in goals, occurring through the individual's response to internal and external changes (Brandtstadter, Wentura, & Greve, 1993). Modifying goals is a means of maximizing satisfaction (Brim, 1992). This modification makes goals more attainable, providing a sense of direction that may minimize depression (Brandstadter, 1992). Eliminating goals entirely was also supported as an option. Possibly having no goals is another strategy people use when facing adversity. This may place the older person in the best position for having a sense of control and mastery over his or her life. This view was supported by findings that personal goals are adjusted to changes in resources and functional capacities among the old.

OTHER FACTORS TO CONSIDER IN THE EXAMINATION OF DEPRESSION

Feelings of depression are likely to occur when goals are not attainable (Pyszczynski & Greenberg, 1992). Research findings show that people who are depressed are more likely to have unattainable goals (Brandtstadter & Baltes-Gotz, 1990; Carver & Scheier, 1990; Pyszczynski & Greenberg, 1992).

Depression is a problem faced by many older people. There is substantial literature identifying factors related to depression. One sixth of the elderly in the United States suffer from clinically significant depressive syndromes (Lebowitz, 1996). Even when symptoms do not meet the DSM-IV criteria for major depression, depressive symptoms are common among the elderly (Unutzer, Katon, Sullivan, & Miranda, 1999). Although there is great variability of prevalence estimates for depression among the old, ranging from 1.6 to 26.9% (Gurland, Cross, & Katz, 1996), there is agreement that the prevalence of major depression is greater in institutional settings (1–3%) as compared with community settings (6–9%). Major depression is greater among women (Linzer et al., 1996; Unutzer, Katon, Sullivan, et al., 1999) and among multiethnic elderly living in poverty in the inner city (Arean, Robinson, & Hicks, 1997).

Older people share many of the risk factors evident in other age groups, such as being female, single, poor, and socially isolated and experiencing depression earlier in life (Ranga et al., 1998). In addition, older people are more likely than other age groups to have risk factors such as loss and grief, caretaking responsibilities, and illness in themselves or a family member (Jorm, 1998; Ormel et al., 1997; Roberts, Kaplan, Shema, & Strawbridge, 1997). For instance, studies showed that the death of a spouse is associated in the remaining spouse with increased mortality due to suicide and other causes (Unutzer, Katon, Sullivan, et al., 1999), as well as an increase in major depression (Jacobs, 1993). With 7% of the American population widowed each year (13 million people) and with the majority of these being older people (Unutzer, Katon, Sullivan, et al., 1999), there is great concern for their mental health. In addition, caregiving responsibility increase with age. The spouse is most often the caregiver with health problems of his or her own that can contribute to depression. When health problems impinge on functional ability, the elder is at greater risk for depression as well (Ormel et al., 1997).

Barriers to care are often faced by older people, especially the very old, ethnic minorities, and those who are poor. (Unutzer, Katon, Sullivan et al., 1999). These barriers are obstacles to setting goals and gaining a sense of control over life. For the very old, further barriers include sensory problems that contribute to lessened ability to follow prescribed treatments; existential challenges (Blazer, 1993) in which older people find no meaning in life and therefore do not pursue treatment options; and cognitive impairment, which may inhibit an individual's capacity to follow treatment regimens or even to be successfully diagnosed (Weiner et al., 1997). Decreased functional ability may result in greater isolation as well. All of these barriers foster depression and in all likelihood diminish the capacity to establish goals.

Other psychological factors such as control or mastery may also play a part in depression among the elderly. Rodin (1986) found that increased opportunity for control and greater mastery have a positive effect on the physical and psychological status of institution-alized elderly. Holahan, Holahan, and Beck (1984) suggested that the same relationship might exist among older people who live in the community. They found less depression associated with perceptions of mastery in dealing with negative life events, such as poorer functioning. Therefore, it suggests that a greater sense of mastery promotes a greater sense of well being and lessened depression.

Self-esteem also plays a key role in depression, acting as a source of motivation for current or future activities (Cantor & Kihlstrom, 1987). It is also central to issues such as goal setting, which involves a capacity for future orientation. Problems of self-esteem may result from experiencing loss such as the death of a spouse or decline in functional ability and thus reduce the likelihood of having goals

This chapter explores goals among the very old. What goals do these very old people have? If they have them, do they have goals consistently? Lastly, what is the relationship between well-being, depression, and goals among these very old people?

Measures

Goals were determined by asking the respondent, "Do you have any particular goals/plans for the next few months?" Demographic, functional, and psychological factors were considered important factors that contribute to the ability to have a future time perspective among those who are very old. Demographic variables included race, gender, socioeconomic status, marital status, and age. Health measures were self-rated health and instrumental and physical functioning. Mental-health measures included well-being and depression; psychological resources were self-esteem and mastery, as well as degree of worry (for greater detail, see the Appendix).

GOALS

Using the open-ended question, "Do you have any particular goals or plans for the next few months," the respondent could identify future goals in whatever context was personally relevant. Two research team members identified coding categories. The responses were then coded independently by two researchers with subsequent discrepancies discussed in order to reach agreement on the classification. Interrater reliability was 0.90. This is well within the minimum standard of 0.80 recommended by Hartmann (1977) and Krippendorff (1980).

Dependent variables were two mental health measures of Bradburn Affect Balance Scale and the Derogotis SCL-90 Depression Scale. The Bradburn Affect Balance Scale is an indicator of general psychological well-being based on the model of two independent factors, negative and positive affect (Bradburn, 1969). The depression index of the Brief Symptom Inventory was used to measure depression in this study (Derogates, 1977). Independent variables included instrumental functioning and physical health functioning. IADLs were measured using the seven items in the Older American Resources and Services Assessment (Duke University, 1978). These include items such as managing finances, using the telephone, and shopping. The Katz Activities of Daily Living Index (Katz, Ford, Moskowitz, Jackson, & Jaffee, 1963) measured activities of daily living, an index measuring the capacity of the individual to be independent in basic tasks of caring for oneself: bathing, dressing, feeding, going to the toilet, and transferring from bed to chair.

There were three psychological measures used: self-esteem, mastery, and worry. Self-esteem was assessed by the Rosenberg Self-Esteem Scale (Rosenberg, 1965). The Pearlin Mastery Scale measured mastery: one factor measured a global sense of control and a second factor, a single item, captured perceived control (greater discussion in chapter 2). A measure of strain was included to determine how much worry these very old people experienced.

Demographic variables included age in years, gender and race, and socioeconomic status, measured using the Hollingshead Two-Factor Index, which considered education and occupation. (For greater detail on all of the measures, see the Appendix.)

KEY FINDINGS

The descriptive information on the sample is presented for those subjects who answered questions at Waves 1 and 2 ($n = 180$) (Table

4.1). As would be expected among a sample age 85 years and older, at Wave 1, 76% of the sample were women and 24% were men and 82.4% were white and 17.6% were black (no other racial or ethnic groups were represented). Of the sample, 77.2% were between the ages of 85 and 89, with 21.2% between 90 and 98 years of age; 70.5% were widowed; and 20.7% were married at Wave 1. Of the participants, 10.9% had 0 to 4 years of formal education, 22.3% had 5 to 8 years of school, 4% had a high-school education, and 15% had some college.

The overall socioeconomic status for the group was lower middle class. Twenty-eight percent were housewives, and 25.4% had been in a service-related occupation. These elders functioned well, scoring high on the IADL scale and the ADL scale. As a group, the subjects had moderate well-being at Wave 1, had moderate scores on mastery and self-esteem at Wave 1, were minimally depressed, and had few worries.

TABLE 4.1   Variable Descriptions*

Name	Mean	S.D.	Theoretical Range	Scoring
Goals (T_1)	—	—	0–1	No/Yes
Goals (T_2)	—	—	0–1	No/Yes
Sex (female)	—	—	0–1	—
Race (white)	—	—	0–1	—
Marital (married)	—	—	0–1	—
SES (T_1)	2.99	1.23	1–5	High = Lower
IADL (T_1)	11.93	1.99	0–14	High = High
ADL (T_1)	11.37	0.97	0–12	High = High
Bradburn (T_1)	6.86	2.06	0–10	High = Positive
Bradburn (T_2)	7.13	2.08	0–10	High = Positive
Mastery (T_1)	12.32	3.47	0–21	High = High
Self-esteem (T_1)	11.49	3.52	1–20	High = High
Depression (T_1)	2.06	2.82	0–24	High = More
Depression (T_2)	2.43	3.09	0–24	High = More
Strain (T_1)	7.09	6.36	0–69	High = More
Self-reported health (T_1)	1.76	0.79	0–3	High = Better

*for 180 subjects at Wave 2 who completed the first two waves of data collection
SD, standard deviation

DO VERY OLD PEOPLE HAVE GOALS?

Most subjects had goals at Wave 1 and Wave 2; 59% of the respondents had goals at Wave 1 and 61% had goals at Wave 2. The distribution of types of goals ranged from being alive to social, recreational, and travel activities (see Table 4.2 for examples). When goals were examined for all five waves (Table 4.3), most subjects had goals for the first four waves. Social activities such as parties, club meetings, and so on, as well as travel and family activities such as births and weddings, were the most common goals that these elders had for the first three waves (Table 4.3). By the fourth wave, 12 (6.2%) were thinking of relocating, usually to be nearer family. This is understandable, because the youngest in the sample was now 87

TABLE 4.2   Example of Types of Goals

Goal (T_1)	Examples
Social activity	Continue doing what I like; 65th reunion at my college; visit relatives in Florida; I am going to the orchestra, plays and the ballet; I have a wedding shower to go to
Recreational	Paint; needlework; church work; crafts; crocheting and knitting
ADL	Keep on living and taking care of myself; do my spring cleaning; work on my houses
Relocation	Selling my house; going to movie; maybe move to a retirement village; get ready to move to a smaller place for financial reasons
Improved health	Get my blood count up; get better, trying to shape up
Death related	Planning my will; want to leave estate to take care of crippled children; plan for future when dead
Family activity	Enjoy my children and grandchildren; grandson getting married; see my brother's grave; niece coming to visit
Travel	When weather is warmer I am going to New York City to see my sister-in-law; going to Greece to see loved one; I'd like to take a day trip with seniors; in October I'd like to go to Guadalajara to visit Lake Chapel
Being alive	To enjoy my life and stay alive; just to live and move and breathe and stay here
Other	Working on my commercial accounts; writing to my senator about the needs of orphaned children

TABLE 4.3 Goals Across the Five Waves

Type	Wave 1		Wave 2		Wave 3		Wave 4		Wave 5	
	n (193)	%	n (180)	%	n (159)	%	n (149)	%	n (21)	%
None	80	41.5	71	36.8	61	31.6	57	29.5	14	66.6
Social activity	22	11.4	20	10.4	5	2.6	5	2.6	1	4.8
Recreational	9	4.7	7	3.6	4	2.1	7	3.6	0	0
ADL	8	4.1	7	3.6	11	5.7	7	3.6	1	4.8
Relocation	6	3.1	10	5.2	9	4.7	12	6.2	1	4.8
Improved health	4	2.1	4	2.1	11	5.7	4	2.1	0	0
Death related	5	2.6	1	.5	1	0.5	1	0.5	0	0
Family activity	13	6.7	12	6.2	18	9.3	9	4.7	3	14.2
Travel	41	21.2	35	18.1	29	15.0	31	16.1	0	0
Being alive	3	1.6	5	2.6	3	1.6	11	5.7	0	0
Other	2	1.0	5	2.6	7	3.6	5	2.6	1	4.8
Missing			3		2		6		2	

years old. At Wave 5 (when the youngest person in the sample was 94 years old), the most frequently mentioned goal for those who had a goal was family activities

By Wave 5, the picture was very different: 66.7% had no goals. Further, the range of codes was narrower than on the first four waves of data (see Table 4.3). Of the 11 coding categories used for the first four waves, only five categories were used in Wave 5 (saying there were no goals was the sixth category). At this point, the elders no longer had goals that included recreation, activities to improve health, travel, being alive, or dying- or death-related activities such as planning a funeral or organizing affairs before death. Many fewer people had goals at Wave 1 (66.7%) compared with Wave 5 (29.8%).

In an effort to determine if goals changed for people over time, we examined goals among the survivors (n = 23) at Waves 1 and 5 (Table 4.4). It should be noted that this survivor group had only seven categories at Wave 1: social activities, ADLs, relocation, family

TABLE 4.4   Goals of Survivors

	Wave 1 ($n = 23$)		Wave 5 ($n = 21$)*	
	n	%	n	%
None	4	17.39	14	66.67
Social activities	5	21.74	1	4.76
Recreation	1	4.35	0	0.00
ADL	2	8.70	1	4.76
Relocation	2	8.70	1	4.76
Improved health	1	4.35	0	0.00
Family activity	1	4.35	3	14.29
Travel	7	30.43	0	0.00
Other	0	0.00	1	4.76

*Two subjects were unable to plan.

activity, recreation, improved health, and travel. The most common goal was travel; examples included "I'm going to Florida next week to visit a friend." "My husband and I will go to Arizona next month." "I'm going to be traveling, going to meetings for my church. We've got a trip in May to Mansfield. I'll be going to a church meeting in Indiana too. I have plans to go to a graduation in New York later." Another said, "I'm going to Pittsburgh through my church organization in a month or so." When describing social activities one respondent said, "the same as every day. We go to dances, play cards and go to lunch." Another said, "I am busy. I have season tickets to the Playhouse, orchestras and ballet." Those who mentioned relocation said, "I've signed up for a retirement home but I'm not sure if I want to go through with it. I really don't want to go there now." One family activity comment was, "I hope to see relatives in New York next month for my birthday." Comments describing recreational activities included, "I'm looking for other things to do in place of the volunteer work that I used to do. If I could work at home, I'd do it." The one person who was looking toward improving her health said, "I just hope everything works out and I get my red blood count up. I think that the iron pills help."

By Wave 5, these 23 people had goals in five categories: social activities, activities of daily living, relocation, family activity, and other. No one had a goal for improving their health, recreation, or travel. Many more people did not have goals at Wave 5 (66.77% as compared with 17.4% at Wave 1). The most common goal was family activity. These results suggest that goals play different roles at different points in the life course and may be varied among the very old.

Correlation results (not shown) revealed that having goals as opposed to not having them at Wave 1 was significantly related to well-being, higher mastery, self-esteem, health, and socioeconomic status, as well as less depression. Having goals at Waves 2, 3, and 4 was significantly related to better IADLs, greater well-being, self-esteem, and more worry. Having goals at Waves 3 and 4 was also significantly related to greater mastery. At Wave 5, having goals was significantly related to better self-rated health.

DO OLDER PEOPLE HAVE GOALS CONSISTENTLY?

The literature on goals and having a future time perspective does not consider the issue of consistency. When someone has future goals, do they always have future goals? Does this consistency have any bearing on their mental health and sense of well-being, as the literature implies that it should? We examined two waves of data 6 months apart at Waves 1 and 2. People who had goals at Wave 1 were more likely to have goals 6 months later. Besides having goals at Wave 1, better IADL ability and greater worry predicted having goals at Wave 2. Considering the things that these subjects listed as goals, such as participation in social activities and travel, it is understandable why their IADL ability was better. The significant relationship between greater worry at Wave 1 and predicting goals at Wave 2 may be due to increasing worry and making plans. Possibly worry motivates the elder to make plans to resolve the worry in the near future. The relationship between higher SES (socio-economic status) and having goals at Wave 2 and lower functional ability (ADL) and having goals at Wave 2 approached statistical significance ($p < 0.10$). Higher socioeconomic status may enable the elder to travel and make social plans, whereas lower functional ability may promote goals related to relocation, affairs related to death, and other events.

Goal Consistency

Having goals was not a consistent pattern between Waves 1 and 2. Not all respondents consistently had goals for their future. To explore this further, four subgroups were constructed: people (1) having goals at both Wave 1 and Wave 2, (2) having no goals at either point, (3) having goals at Wave 1 and not at Wave 2, and (4) not having goals at Wave 1 but having them at Wave 2. Only 41% of the respondents had goals at Waves 1 and 2 as compared with 24.4% who had no goals at either wave; 12.4% had goals at Wave 1 but not at Wave 2; and 14% had goals at Wave 2 but not at Wave 1. Those who had goals at Wave 1 were more likely to have them at Wave 2.

The kind of goals the participants had also varied depending on goal pattern. People who had goals at both times had goals in all categories, with travel being the most common goal at Wave 1 (35.4%) and at Wave 2 (34.2%). Those who had goals at Wave 1 but not 6 months later at Wave 2, had only 5 types of goals out of the 11 possible types (social activities, ADL abilities, improved health, family activities, and travel, with the most prevalent category once again being travel [41.7%]). Those elders who did not have goals at Wave 1 but did have them at Wave 2 had goals that covered 8 categories: social activity, recreation, ADL abilities, relocation, improved health, family activities, travel, and being alive. Once again, the most common goal was travel (29.6%).

We also examined consistency for each survivor. Only four respondents had no goals at Wave 1, but this did not mean that they had no goals at Waves 2 and 5. In fact, of these four people, only one consistently had no goals. Through the first 6 months of the study (Waves 1 and 2), the survivors actively identified goals. By Wave 5, most respondents had no future time perspective anymore. When asked if she had any goals in the next 6 months, one woman said, "I take it as it comes." Many others were focused on the present. One woman said, "I have no plans—just to get up the next day and cook and eat." Another said "just marking time," and another said "I just keep going and moving and hoping for no problems."

It was important to determine whether health or demographic factors explained why subjects had these various goal patterns. We looked more closely at the characteristics of the goal combination subgroups and the variables in this study using analysis of variance.

These four groups were not significantly different from one another on most measures. Differences did exist with self-rated health and well-being. The group that had goals at both time points scored significantly higher on self-rated health at Wave 1 and well-being at Waves 1 and 2 than did the group that had no goals either time. There were no significant differences among the four groups on measures of self-esteem, depression, mastery, IADL, and ADL. Possibly feeling positive about life and feeling that your health is good encouraged the elder to look to the future and make plans.

THE RELATIONSHIP BETWEEN MENTAL HEALTH AND HAVING GOALS

First we looked at the relationship between mental health measures (well-being and depression) and demographic, health, and psychological measures for these very old subjects at Wave 1 and also looked at predicting change in depression and well-being at Wave 2. Different factors were related to well-being and depression at Wave 1. Less worry and better self-rated health significantly predicted well-being at Wave 1. Being older, worrying more, and having lower self-esteem significantly predicted depression at Wave 1. Having goals was not predictive of mental health in the present (when all measures were taken in the same wave of data). Possibly having goals promotes a sense of well-being or lessens depression in the future.

When examining depression at Wave 2, goals at Wave 1 had no significant relationship to depression either, but increasing age and increasing worry were significantly related; being black and of lower socioeconomic status were marginally significant ($p \leq 0.10$). None of these measures predicted well-being at Wave 2 except for the elder's well-being at Wave 1. The goal pattern subgroups were also examined to determine if consistency of having goals predicted less depression and greater well-being at the second wave. In these ordinary least squares (OLS) regression equations, we also controlled for the Wave 1 measure of the dependent variable (depression/well-being) in order to eliminate the possibility that depression or well-being at Wave 1 accounted for depression or well-being at Wave 2.

Four dummy variables representing four different patterns of goals were entered into the two OLS equations (Table 4.5). The dummy

TABLE 4.5   Ordinary Least Squares Regression of Change in Well-Being on Goals, Social, Psychological, and Demographic Factors

Variables	Step 1 Beta	Step 2 Beta	Step 1 R^2	Step 2 R^2
Bradburn (W1)	0.651[*]	0.543[*]	0.651[*]	0.72
Sex (female)		0.013		
Race (white)		−0.064		
Marital (married)		0.056		
Age (W1)		−0.020		
Health (W1)		0.086		
Goals at W1 and W2		0.152[**]		
Goals at W2		−0.013		
Goals at W1		−0.079		
SES (W1)		0.051[**]		
IADL (W1)		−0.109		
ADL (W1)		0.036		
Mastery (W1)				
Global		0.157[*]		
Perceived control		−0.044		
Self-esteem (W1)		0.026		
Strain (W1)		−0.076		

[*] $p < 0.000$
[**] $p < 0.05$

variables include, first, having goals at one time point or the other or having goals at both time points, with the reference category as having no goals at Wave 1 and Wave 2. When change in well-being at Wave 2 was examined, greater well-being at Wave 1 and having goals at both Wave 1 and Wave 2 as compared with having no goals at either time point were significant predictors of greater well-being at Wave 2 (Table 4.5). Lower SES and greater sense of mastery at Wave 1 were also related to better well-being at Wave 2. Lower well-being at Wave 2 existed for the group that did not have goals at either time point and the group that had goals at Wave 1 but not at Wave 2 as compared with those respondents who had goals at both time points (yes/yes) (tables not shown). Over all, having consistent goals over a 6-month period related to greater well-being at Wave 2.

Several factors predicted greater depression at Wave 2: greater depression at Wave 1, younger age, and greater worry, as well as the goal pattern in which the subjects had goals at Wave 1 but not at Wave 2 (as compared with those who had no goals at either wave) (Table 4.6). Closer examination of the various goal combinations showed that there was less depression at Wave 2 for the group that had goals at both waves and the group that never had goals as compared with the group that had goals at Wave 1 but not Wave 2 (tables not shown).

In summary, having goals was significantly related to mental health measures when examined in bivariate relationships. When demographic and psychological factors were also considered, goals were not important when predicting mental health at the same time point or 6 months later. The important finding is related to the consistency of having goals. The subjects who had greater well-being at Wave 2 were the ones who had goals at both Wave 1 and Wave 2 as compared

TABLE 4.6 Ordinary Least Squares Regression of Change in Depression on Goals, Social, Psychological, and Demographic Factors

Variables	Step 1 Beta	Step 2 Beta	Step 1 R^2	Step 2 R^2
Depression (W1)	0.61^*	0.435^*	0.61^*	0.71
Sex (female)		0.033		
Race (white)		0.111		
Goals at W1 and W2		0.070		
Goals at W1 only		0.196^{**}		
Goals at W2 only		0.081		
Marital (married)		-0.043		
Age (W1)		-0.132^{**}		
Health (W1)		0.000		
SES (W1)		0.093		
IADL (W1)		-0.052		
ADL (W1)		-0.045		
Mastery (W1)				
Global		-0.096		
Perceived		-0.017		
Self-esteem (W1)		-0.036		
Strain (W1)		0.227^{**}		

$^*p < 0.000$
$^{**}p < 0.01$
$^{***}p < 0.05$

with those who had no goals at either time. Other goal patterns were not significant. Greater depression at Wave 2 was related to being younger and worrying more, as well as having the inconsistent goal pattern of goals at Wave 1 but not at Wave 2, as compared with those who had no goals either time. It seems that it is the inconsistent pattern that introduces a sense of loss of control (having goals and then not having goals) and is related to greater depression, rather than either consistently having goals or not having goals at both time points.

Well-being seems to operate differently, for it is only the group that had goals at both waves that had significantly better well-being when compared with those who had no goals either wave. Inconsistent patterns, having goals at only one wave, are insignificant with regard to well-being.

DISCUSSION

Most very old people have a variety of goals; they had a future time perspective, thus supporting the findings of Smith and Baltes (1999). Unlike the work of Johnson and Barer (1997), who found that these very old people were oriented to the present, the findings in this study only found a preponderance of this at Wave 5, when the youngest subject was 94 years of age. Most of our very old subjects had goals for the first 18 months of the study. Seven years later (at Wave 5), only 30% of the survivors had goals. The range of goals varied, with the survivors having a more limited range of goals. In particular, they no longer looked forward to recreation or travel or even dying or staying alive. Rather, their goals involved social activities, family activities, and performing everyday functional tasks. In some cases, the goals also involved looking toward relocating.

Goal identification exists in very late life for a subgroup of the sample (30%), underscoring the grasp on control that some very old people maintain, even if in a modified manner as time progressed. As death approached, some of these survivors, those that were interviewed at Wave 5, still had goals, although it is important to recognize that most no longer did. As suggested by Carstensen and Freund (1994), there seems to be a restriction of the person's personal projection into the future among the survivors who were in their mid-90s.

It is unclear why there is a reduction in range of goals and number of people who had goals. There seems to be a cohort effect; the survivors at Wave 5 had fewer different types of goals even at Wave 1 than had the remainder of the sample. Poorer health and functioning at Wave 5 may account for a narrower range of goals as well. Possibly, specific goals may be more prominent at certain times during the life span (Carstensen & Freund, 1994). Goals could also reflect changes in resources and functional capacity (Brandtstadter, Wentura, & Greve, 1993).

Although most of these very old people had goals at the beginning of the study, the majority did not have them consistently. It is unclear what accounts for these goal patterns. Better health and well-being were the only measures that significantly differentiated those who had goals at both points from those who did not have goals either time. For the other pattern, having goals at one time or the other, there were no significant differences in health, functioning, or psychological resources.

We did find interesting relationships between goals and the mental health measures of well-being and depression. Subjects who had goals at both times had significantly better health and well-being as compared with those who did not have goals at either time. Goal inconsistency, on the other hand, was the goal pattern that was significantly related to greater depression 6 months later. People who had goals at Wave 1 but not at Wave 2 were more depressed than were those who did not have goals either time.

As Rodin (1986) suggests, having less control has a negative effect on mental health. Not having goals after having goals possibly represents a loss of control for the elder and results in depression, unlike the effect of not having goals at all. Those who had no goals either time may never have had goals and therefore may not have experienced a change in an anticipated future. The result may be better mental health (Diener, 1984; Holahan, 1988). One explanation may be summed up by Nuttin's view that in the face of adversity or circumstances in which the future is unpredictable, people are less likely to have goals.

Unfortunately, this study did not ascertain whether the goals these elders identified were ever achieved. This is an important dimension in understanding goals and their relationship to control and mental health and a very important research topic to pursue in gaining greater understanding of the future time perspective of the very old.

CHAPTER 5

Coping in Late Life

The adverse effects of stress on mental health are well-known (Aldwin, Levenson, Spiro, & Bosse, 1984; Blazer, Hughes, & George, 1987; Krause, 1986; Krause, 1987b), and coping resources are essential to mitigate these effects. Past experiences in coping with stressful situations are used to select coping strategies for current stress. Coping has been found to significantly predict perceived negative and positive outcomes of stress (Aldwin, Sutton, & Lachman, 1996), and some types of coping have been associated with mental health (Burke & Flaherty, 1993; Pruchno, Burant, & Peters, 1997), whereas others have been associated with depression (Coyne, Aldwin, & Lazarus, 1999; Folkman, Lazarus, Dunkel-Schetter, DeLonges, & Gruen, 1986).

Stress taxes or threatens resources available to meet these challenges of life (George, 1989; Lazarus & Folkman, 1984). One type of stress is life events that are discrete with subsequent but not necessarily lasting effects (Holmes & Rahe, 1967). Worry, on the other hand, is comprised of daily hassles that are enduring and represent daily worries or concerns (DeLongis, Cohen, Dakof, Folkman, & Lazarus, 1982; Kessler, 1983; Lazarus & Folkman, 1984). The very old may have different types of stress and resources to cope than younger adults (Costa & McCrae, 1993). Little is known about the kinds of stress experienced by the very old and the coping resources they use in dealing with stress.

Worry has a greater impact on depression and mental health than stressful life events (DeLongis et al., 1982; Holahan, Holahan, & Belk, 1984; Kanner, Coyne, Schaefer, & Lazarus, 1981; Roberts, Dunkle, et al., 1994; Weinberger, Hiner, & Tierney, 1985). Whether these differences in the impact of worry and life events are associated with other aspects of mental health has received little attention (Roberts, Dunkle, et al., 1994).

In the transaction model of stress (Chiriboga, 1992), the environment influences the person and vice versa (Lazarus & Launier, 1978). Stress can best be understood as a transaction of stressful life events and daily challenges with resources to prevent their adverse effects. The transactional model is process oriented, allowing for the examination of the coping resources actually used and focusing on actual behavior and its consequences.

An individual appraises situations as stressful when they are beyond the context of self-perceptions and the resources available to meet these challenges. Hence, not all life events or daily hassles are perceived as stressful. At the psychological level, the individual uses appraisal to give meaning to a particular situation. Appraisal involves evaluation of what is at stake and the resources at hand to manage the situation (Folkman et al., 1986; Lazarus & Folkman, 1984). Appraisal thus serves as the pathway through which personal and environmental variables influence the outcomes of stressful events. Psychological characteristics influence the appraisal process by predisposing the individual to perceive events as threatening or not (Folkman et al., 1986). Mastery and self-esteem are important psychological characteristics against which individuals appraise their situations and resources (Krause, 1987a, b, c).

The individual then appraises the availability of resources to meet these challenges and mobilizes them to mitigate or resolve the stresses and worries of life. Social support, mastery, and coping are the most important (Krause, 1987 a, b); self-esteem may also be a resource (Krause, 1987c). Appraisal is also used to assess the usefulness of various coping strategies to manage environmental and internal demands (Folkman et al., 1986; Lazarus & Folkman, 1984).

The coping process requires changes in the environment that subsequently influence future behavior. The outcome of the interaction between stress and personal resources results in adaptation. Coping in the presence of stress has been conceptualized as moderating the effects of stress on mental health (George, 1989; Revicki & Mitchell, 1990; Roberts, Dunkle, et al., 1994) and as a mediator of stress (Lazarus & Folkman, 1984). The moderating and mediating effects of coping strategies on the relationship between stress and mental health have not been consistently found (Roberts, Dunkle, et al., 1994).

In the transaction model of stress, the person influences the environment and vice versa. The mediating and moderating nature of coping resources and their effects in mitigating the negative effects of stress have been studied. In the mediator model, stress mobilizes resources that have a direct effect on mental health. That is, resources have a mediating effect, whereas stress has an indirect effect on mental health. In the moderator model, these personal resources mitigate the relationship between stress and mental health. Little research has focused on the role of psychosocial and physical resources in managing stress among the oldest-old. Support for these models has been inconsistent and has varied depending on the stressful situation.

In this chapter, the stress experienced by the very old, coping strategies, and coping resources are described. The relationships of stress to mental health and coping resources are described, and the mediator and moderator models of stress are assessed. Comparisons are made between those who survived to be interviewed 9 years after the initial interview and those who survived to be interviewed at Wave 4, 18 months after the initial interview. To facilitate reporting results for these subgroups, the same nomenclature for the subgroups used in chapter 2 will be used here. Although respondents were interviewed every 6 months (Waves 1 to 4), only Waves 1 and 4 are used because the 18 months between these two data points were needed for substantial change to emerge.

STRESSORS AND WORRIES

Although there has been extensive research regarding stress, little is known about stress among the very old (Roberts, Dunkle, et al., 1994). The number of roles these individuals engage in is less than that for younger adults. The decline in the number of roles may reduce the stressors encountered. In contrast, the very old often are confronted with many personal and social losses that may alter the stresses they encounter and reduce their access to supportive networks (Caldwell & Reinhart, 1988). Poor health and disability may be sources of stress because of their effects on quality of life and performance of daily activities.

Stressors

Stressors are discrete life events that have subsequent but not necessarily lasting effects (Kessler, 1983; Pearlin et al., 1981) and were measured by the Geriatric Scale of Recent Life Events (Kahana, Fairchild, & Kahana, 1982). The respondents indicated those events that had occurred in the last year.

Wave 5 survivors did not have a greater number of negative or positive life events at baseline or 18 months later than those who were only interviewed at baseline or those who were Wave 4 survivors. (See chapter 2 for a summary of these three groups.) An inclusive description of these events is summarized in Table 5.1.

The most frequent life events experienced by respondents were related to their health. Although less than 15% in all subgroups had experienced a major illness, a significant proportion of the respondents reported functional difficulties. For example, approximately half experienced difficulty walking at Wave 1, whereas many had recent losses in vision and hearing with smaller proportions experiencing poorer sleep and changes in eating. These events reflect significant recent changes in health and function that may have made daily activities more difficult and may have led to changes in driving and residence.

At Waves 1 and 4, approximately one third of the respondents experienced the recent illness of a family member, and about 20% had a family member die. The respondents' social network of friends was also diminished, with nearly 40% of the respondents reporting a death of a friend. However, these losses were offset with marriages and birth of children. These life events were accompanied by a reduced number of religious and family activities, with one fifth of the respondents traveling less.

TABLE 5.1 Percentage and Frequencies of Life Events Among the Old-est-Old

Life Event	Baseline			18 Months Later	
	Did not live to Wave 4 (*n* = 38)	Lived to Wave 4 but not to Wave 5 (*n* = 131)*	Lived to Wave 5 (*n* = 23)	Lived to Wave 4 but not to Wave 5 (*n* = 131)	Lived to Wave 5 (*n* = 23)
Health and Function					
Major illness	13.2 (5)†	15.3 (20)	13.0 (3)	13.8 (18)	0.0 (0)
Significant injury	15.8 (6)	12.2 (16)	21.7 (5)	5.4 (7)	4.3 (1)
Difficulty walking	52.6 (20)	55.7 (73)	43.5 (10)	57.7 (75)	39.1 (9)
Vision loss	31.6 (12)	40.5 (53)	39.1 (9)	40.8 (53)	47.8 (11)
Hearing loss	28.9 (11)	36.6 (48)	26.1 (6)	34.6 (45)	30.4 (7)
Poorer sleep	18.4 (7)	23.7 (31)	21.7 (5)	20.8 (27)	21.7 (5)
Change in eating	28.9 (11)	20.6 (27)	13.0 (3)	22.3 (29)	17.4 (4)
Significant Others					
Illness of family member	26.3 (10)	40.5 (53)	26.1 (6)	31.5 (41)	34.8 (8)
Death of family member	28.9 (11)	28.5 (37)	17.4 (4)	19.2 (25)	13.0 (3)
Death of friend	47.4 (18)	37.4 (49)	47.8 (11)	32.3 (42)	47.8 (11)
Child born in family	0.0 (0)	27.7 (47)	47.8 (11)	28.5 (37)	21.7 (5)
Marriage in family	18.4 (7)	23.7 (31)	21.7 (5)	16.9 (22)	21.7 (5)
Social Activities					
Reduced church activities	34.2 (13)	23.7 (31)	21.7 (5)	16.2 (21)	4.3 (1)
Reduced frequencies of family activities	10.5 (4)	15.3 (20)	4.3 (1)	16.2 (21)	17.4 (4)
Reduced travel	23.7 (9)	19.1 (25)	21.7 (5)	23.8 (31)	8.7 (2)
Change in recreation	2.6 (1)	10.7 (14)	4.3 (1)	13.1 (17)	21.7 (5)
Other					
Sold car	0.0 (0)	3.8 (5)	0.0 (0)	2.3 (3)	4.3 (1)
Stopped driving	5.3 (2)	6.9 (9)	0.0 (0)	8.5 (11)	13.0 (3)
Sold house	0.0 (0)	0.8 (1)	0.0 (0)	3.1 (4)	8.7 (2)
Changed residence	2.6 (1)	3.1 (4)	0.0 (0)	6.9 (9)	8.7 (2)

(continued)

TABLE 5.1   *(continued)*

Life Event	Baseline			18 Months Later	
	Did not live to Wave 4 (*n* = 38)	Lived to Wave 4 but not to Wave 5 (*n* = 131)*	Lived to Wave 5 (*n* = 23)	Lived to Wave 4 but not to Wave 5 (*n* = 131)	Lived to Wave 5 (*n* = 23)
Change in financial status	7.9 (3)	14.5 (19)	0.0 (0)	13.8 (18)	8.7 (2)
Give up control of money	0.0 (0)	.8 (1)	0.0 (0)	5.4 (7)	0.0 (0)

*Respondents who were interviewed at Wave 4 minus those who were interviewed at Wave 5 (154–23)
†% (frequency)
Note: Life events were not measured at Wave 5
None of the differences between the groups was significant

Although the proportion of respondents experiencing life events provides information about stressors experienced, no information was available about how difficult it was to adjust to these events. However, respondents were asked what the most difficult event that they had experienced was. At the initial interview, 10 to 20% of the respondents reported that no life event was more difficult than any other. However, 18 months later, the proportion of subjects reporting this had increased to 41% for Wave 4 survivors and 29% for Wave 5 survivors. At the initial interview, the most frequent difficult change was death of a significant other for all groups of respondents. At Wave 4, fewer reported this event, and this may be explained by the slightly fewer deaths of family members at Wave 4 (see Table 5.1 for a summary of these deaths).

The next most frequent difficult event was loss of physical capabilities and function. Those with a recent loss of vision, difficulty walking, or a major illness also identified loss of physical capabilities and function as the most difficult change (25%). Those not experiencing these health-related problems cited this as most difficult less frequently (18.3%; χ^2 (df = 2) = 11.3, $p < 0.05$). However, the same was not true for a recent major illness, for which approximately 20%

identified loss of physical capabilities and function as the most difficult (χ^2 (df = 2) = 0.7, $p > 0.05$). Because a decline in physical
capabilities and function may be accompanied with greater dependency on others, it is not surprising that less than 5% of those
who died before Wave 4 and Wave 5 interviews identified loss of
independence as the most difficult change. The proportions were
similar at Wave 4 (2.6 and 4.8%, respectively). In contrast, no one
who survived to Wave 5 reported such a loss as the most difficult
change, even though the loss had occurred.

In summary, life events cited most often were related to health,
physical capabilities, and loss of significant others, which are similar
to life events found difficult by others (Hughes, Blazer, & George,
1988; Lazarus & DeLonges, 1983). Given the advanced age of the
respondents, these events are not unexpected, and they may con-
strain the physical and social resources the oldest-old have available
to deal with others stressors and worries as well as daily activities
(Roberts, Dunkle, et al., 1994).

These results must be interpreted with caution because a number
of methodological issues in the measurement of stress affect the
interpretation of the findings. The measurement strategy assumed
that there would be a dose effect of stressful life events (Kessler,
1997). That is, a greater number of events would mean that the
stress was greater. Although the events selected represented those
that may be most prevalent among the very old, some events may
have been inadvertently omitted.

The checklist of stressful life events used in our study assumes
that each event is similarly stressful for all people. Yet this may not
be the case. Death of a spouse after a long progressive debilitating
illness may be less stressful than is a sudden traumatic death. Positive
life events also have been found to be less stressful than are negative
ones (Zautra & Reich, 1983). The checklist approach to life events
does not disentangle the event from the degree of stress associated
with it (Kessler, 1997).

The checklist strategy also does not allow for the consideration
of other factors that contribute to the degree of stress associated
with the event. Thoits (1983) demonstrated that loss, threat, and
control over the consequences of the event moderate the effects of
stress on mental health. For example, death of a spouse with a large
pension may be more stressful for a spouse with very limited pension

or social security than it is for a spouse with greater financial reserves and income.

The reliability of the checklist strategy for the measurement of life events depends on the accuracy of the recall of the events. Some respondents may not want to disclose some events; others may have been forgotten. Among the very old, cognitive abilities may also bias the recall of stressful life events. Short-term memory is more impaired in dementia and may be the first sign of this illness. Moreover, delirium is associated with varying difficulties with memory. Hence, the very old respondent might be able to recall an event from last week today but not be able to remember it tomorrow. Although the respondents in our study were cognitively intact at the time of the interview, subtle problems with memory may still have gone unnoticed and reduced the accuracy of the reporting of stressful life events.

Intensive interviews, in which recall of events is dated by other occurrences (e.g., holiday, seasons of the year, birth of a child), increase the accuracy of recall (Sobell, Toneatto, Sobell, Schuller, & Maxwell, 1990). However, these interviews are very time consuming, and the coding schemes are very complex, requiring extensive training (Wallston, Brown, Stein, & Dobbins, 1989). The interviews also do not allow for separating the stressful event from other modifying factors because these are used in assigning a rating for the stressful event (Kessler, 1997).

Interviews with informants are a means to corroborate the presence of stressful life events. However, reporting recall is a biasing factor with these informants as well. Because the majority of family and friends with knowledge of these events were old or very old, similar factors affecting the recall of these events for the very old respondents may have also been present. Moreover, informants may not be aware of all the stressful life events that the respondents have experienced (Kessler, 1997).

Kessler (1997) noted that stressful life events may not be random, and statistical control of confounding factors may not adequately adjust for these factors. Depression can influence the number of stressful life events recalled. For example, in experimental research, depressed mood increased the number of stressful life events recalled (Cohen, Towbes, & Flocco, 1988). Recent work suggests that a genetic vulnerability to depression increases the recall of stressful life events (Kendler, Kessler, Heath, & Eaves, 1993; Kessler, Kendler, Heath, Neale, & Eaves, 1992). History of depression is a significant predictor of depression with a stressful life event. For example, Robins and Reiger (1991) found that almost all respondents with depression had a history of depression. Moreover, this history was related to factors thought to modify stress (Kessler & Magee, 1994).

Disentangling these measurement and methodological issues is the focus of ongoing research. New methodologies and statistical analyses are needed (Kessler, 1997). The results about stressful life events from our study should be interpreted with these caveats in mind.

Worries

Worries are hassles that are enduring and encountered on a daily basis, and they were measured by the modified Hassles Scale (Kanner et al., 1981). A checklist of conditions that make everyday activities difficult and stressful is based on the assumption of a dose effect of these stressful ongoing conditions. Although there has been some suggestion that these items are confounded with psychopathology, evidence to the contrary has been found (Lazarus, DeLongis, Folkman, & Gruen, 1985). (See Roberts, Dunkle, et al., 1994 for a discussion of these issues.) The measurement issues related to stressful life events are salient to the measurement of worry. As for stressful life events, the following results about worry must be interpreted with caution.

At the initial interview, overall worry was low, averaging approximately 6.0 (out of a maximum of 69) for the three groups of respondents. Worry significantly increased at Wave 4. Among Wave 5 survivors, worry also significantly increased from the initial interview to Wave 5 (see chapter 2 for a summary).

Perhaps the increasing dependence in ADLs and effects of chronic health conditions have made completing everyday tasks difficult resulting in chronic worry. The data regarding individual worries provide beginning support for this hypothesis.

Most worries were related to health and function. The most frequent concerns were related to falls, not enough energy, forgetting things, ability to get around, and health in general. Interestingly,

Wave 5 survivors had fewer worries regarding their health than did Wave 4 survivors and those only interviewed at baseline. Although few in number, similar proportions of the three groups of respondents worried a great deal about their health. However, fewer Wave 5 survivors worried about falls at Wave 1 than did members of the other two subgroups of respondents. Except for Wave 5 survivors, the proportion concerned about falls were similar to the percentage of independent living adults 65 and older expressing a fear of falling (Arfkin, Lash, Birge, & Miller, 1994; Howland, Peterson, Levin, Fried, Pordon, & Bak, 1993; Tinetti, DeLeon, Doucette, & Baker, 1994). Worry related to declining strength increased significantly between Wave 1 and 5. Similar patterns of increasing worry were found for physical abilities, health, energy, and others related to physical and cognitive abilities. Clearly, health and impaired physical abilities presented the very old with chronic worries (see Table 5.2 for a summary).

The most frequent worry was not related to health and capabilities but to the health of a family member, with approximately 40% experiencing this worry. Other worries increased in frequency between Waves 1 and 4. At the 18-month interview, the most frequent concerns of respondents were about adequacy of financial resources and physical appearance.

At the last interview, respondents experienced worry in all items measured. In prior interviews, Wave 5 survivors had significantly fewer concerns about their health and declining strength and, hence, concomitantly fewer worries related to poorer physical abilities, getting around, and falling. As those who did not survive to the last interview, Wave 5 survivors had similar worries related to insufficient energy for daily tasks, misplacing things and forgetfulness.

Although respondents rated their health as good and used few health-care resources, many required assistance with ADLs and IADLs (see chapter 2), which may have made completing necessary daily tasks difficult and may have contributed to the worry related to physical and cognitive abilities. To test this hypothesis, the health of Wave 4 and 5 survivors was assessed. Compared with Wave 4 survivors, Wave 5 survivors were significantly more independent in ADLs ($M = 11.4$ and 11.7, respectively; t [189] = 2.9, $p < 0.01$) and IADLs ($M = 11.8$ and 13.2, respectively; t [189] = 4.6, $p < 0.001$). Yet, both Wave 4 and Wave 5 survivors rated their health as fair.

TABLE 5.2 Worries of the Oldest-Old

Worries	Baseline			18 Months Later		9 Years Later
	Did not live to Wave 4 (n = 38)	Lived to Wave 4 but not to Wave 5 (n=131)*	Lived to Wave 5 (n = 23)	Lived to Wave 4 but not to Wave 5 (n=131)	Lived to Wave 5 (n = 23)	Lived to Wave 5 (n = 23)
Worry about health	31.6 (12)†	27.8 (47)	17.4 (4)	40.8 (51)	21.7 (5)	100 (23)
Less physical abilities	15.8 (6)	18.3 (31)	13.3 (3)	43.2 (54)	30.4 (7)	100 (23)
Not enough energy	23.7 (9)	32.5 (55)	30.4 (7)	48.0 (60)	43.5 (10)	100 (23)
Declining strength	13.2 (5)	14.2 (24)	4.3 (1)	44.8 (56)	26.1 (6)	100 (23)
Worry about getting around	21.1 (8)	27.2 (56)	17.4 (4)	37.6 (48)	21.7 (4)	100 (23)
Worry about falling	39.5 (15)	39.6 (67)	17.4 (4)	53.6 (67)	34.8 (8)	100 (23)
Worry about forgetting things	36.8 (14)	36.1 (61)	30.4 (7)	46.0 (57)	43.5 (10)	100 (23)
Misplace or lose things	28.9 (11)	29.0 (49)	26.1 (6)	32.8 (41)	45.5 (10)	100 (23)
Worry about health of a family member	44.7 (17)	46.2 (78)	52.2 (12)	40.8 (61)	39.1 (9)	100 (23)
Worry about physical appearance	2.6 (1)	6.3 (12)	13.0 (3)	34.7 (51)	26.1 (6)	100 (23)
Concerns about money	13.2 (5)	8.3 (16)	8.7 (2)	22.4 (28)	17.4 (4)	100 (23)
Too much time on hands	10.5 (4)	18.9 (32)	13.0 (2)	26.4 (43)	17.4 (4)	100 (23)

*Respondents who were interviewed at Wave 4 minus those who were interviewed at Wave 5 (154–23)
†% (frequency)
Note: None of the differences between the groups was significant

This hypothesis is further supported by the relationship of health preventing the respondent from engaging in tasks and activities. At Wave 1, 50% of those who stated that health interfered with activities also indicated that they had worry related to lower physical abilities, 46.5% had trouble getting around, and 47.7% did not have enough energy (all χ^2 (df = 2), $p < 0.01$). Similar findings were found for Wave 4. These findings suggest that health concerns prevented many respondents from engaging in activities and added to the daily worries of their lives.

In summary, the greatest worries were related to health and dependency in daily activities, which are findings similar to others (Folkman, Lazarus, Pimley, & Novacek, 1987). Respondents who identified these types of worries also stated that health interfered with activities. Although disability and health are not the same, they may both impede the performance of daily activities and contribute to the ongoing daily worry of life. The health-related worries might consume an inordinate amount of coping resources that diminish the ability of the oldest-old to cope with stressful life events.

RELATIONSHIP OF STRESS TO PHYSICAL AND MENTAL HEALTH

Physical Health

Selye (1956) and Holmes and Rahe (1967) hypothesized that stress would have adverse effects on physical health. Selye (1956) demonstrated a relationship with physical stressors, but Holmes and Rahe (1967) were the first to suggest that stressful life events would have a similar impact on health. Recently, negative events were significantly related to greater serum prolactin; blood pressure and serum triglycerides also increased with these events (Theorell & Emlund, 1993). These physiological changes contribute to cardiovascular disease, which is very prevalent in the very old.

In spite of physiological changes, the deleterious effects of stress on physical health are not found consistently. For example, in men, the relationship of negative life events to physical health was extremely small (Cui & Vaillant, 1996). In young men, negative life events were related to illness, whereas positive life events were not (Sarason, Sarason, Potter, & Antoni, 1985). Others found that stress increased the susceptibility of developing a cold (Cohen, Tyrell, & Smith, 1993).

In our study, the development of acute illnesses and new chronic diseases were not assessed, but perception of health was measured from 0 "poor" to 4 "excellent." Although disease and acute illness vary considerably in severity, the interference of these in performance of daily activities depends to a certain extent on the severity of illness. To capture this interference, ADLs and IADLs were measured, along with perceptions of the degree to which illness interfered with activities (1 "never" to 3 "often").

Greater life events and worry were related to perceptions of poorer health, but these relationships, although significant, were small ($r = -0.18$ and -0.28, respectively; $p < 0.01$). As the number of life events and worry increased, the interference of health in performing activities increased ($r = 0.31$ and 0.42, respectively; $p < 0.0001$). As found by others (Sarason et al., 1985), positive life events were not significantly related to perceived health or interference with activities ($r < 0.16$). In contrast, the effects of negative life events were small for perceived health but were greater for interference with activities ($r = 0.32$, $p < 0.0001$). The difference in the effects of stress on these perceptions may be explained by the differential influence of disease on activities and general health. Although health may be poor, its effects on performing daily activities may present the very old with daily challenges that make negative life events more difficult to manage. This may explain why the relationship was stronger for interference with engaging in activities and negative events than it was for perceptions of health in general and negative events.

Poorer health may contribute to greater dependence in ADL and IADL, and similar relationships between them and stress would be expected. Although the relationships of worry to ADLs and IADLs were significant at the initial interview, they were small ($r = -0.16$ and -0.18, respectively), as were the relationships to life events ($r < -0.04$). Although negative life events had little impact on the performance of these daily activities ($r < 0.08$ for both types of activities), positive life events were weakly associated with ADLs ($r = -0.16$) and negligibly associated with IADL ($r = 0.08$).

Mental Health

Older adults experience poorer mental health with stress (Aldwin et al., 1989; Aldwin & Revenson, 1986; Blazer et al., 1987; Holahan et al., 1984; Krause, 1987a, b; Roberts, Dunkle, et al., 1994). The effects of negative life events are more strongly associated with mental health (Krishnan et al., 1998; Penninx et al., 1998) than are positive events (Krishnan et al., 1998). In contrast to life events, worry has a much greater influence on mental health (DeLongis et al., 1982; Holahan et al., 1984; Kanner et al., 1981; Roberts, Dunkle, et al., 1994).

At Wave 1, greater negative life events were not significantly related to poorer general mental health, greater depression ($r < 0.16$), or general well-being assessed by the Bradburn Affect Balance Scale ($r = -0.06$). Similarly, positive life events had negligible associations with rating of mental health ($r < 0.1$) and general mental health ($r = -0.10$). At baseline, worry was strongly related to depression ($r = 0.55$) but less so to ratings of poorer mental health ($r = -0.20$) and general mental health ($r = -0.34$).

Several factors may account for inconsistencies between these findings and those of others. Prior investigators studied a very limited number of very old adults and did not compare them with younger cohorts. Older adults refer to past stressful experiences to select coping strategies for current stressors (Aldwin et al., 1996). The few who live to very old age may have a greater wealth of effective coping strategies to draw upon than have younger cohorts, few of whom will live into their 80s.

Although the relationship between stress and mental health was assessed, dependence in ADLs and poor physical health may explain some of the findings because they have been associated with depression and poorer mental health (Bienenfeld et al., 1997). Those who have survived to old age, such as those in our study, may have been more physically vigorous and, in the past, may have more effectively approached the challenges of life. Greater independence in daily activities may provide the oldest-old with greater capabilities to meet the challenges of life (Roberts, Dunkle, et al., 1994). Poor physical health may make managing daily activities difficult because more energy may be required to do them. Little energy or time may be available for coping with stressful life events and worry, thus allowing their negative effects on mental health to accumulate. Recently, there was some support for this hypothesis. Russell and Cutrona (1991) found that ADLs, IADLs, and negative life events significantly contributed to worry (daily hassles) and have been associated with greater depression (DeLongis et al., 1982; Holahan et al., 1984; Kanner et al., 1981).

COPING RESOURCES

Coping resources are used to attenuate the effects of stress and include strategies to resolve stressful situations or manage emotional reactions to them. Psychological and social resources have been found to mediate the effects of stress on mental health and moderate the relationship between stress and mental health (Roberts, Dunkle, et al., 1994). These resources include mastery, self-esteem (Kessler, 1997; Roberts, Dunkle, et al., 1994), and social support (Roberts, Anthony, et al., 1994). Persons with ineffective coping strategies and few psychological and social resources will suffer (Roberts, Dunkle, et al., 1994).

Coping Strategies

People use an array of coping strategies that can be tailored to a certain situation (Krause, 1987a; Krause, 1987b), and individuals may have a predominant coping style. Coping strategies require the individual to mobilize resources, perceptions, and actions needed to mitigate stress. Emotion-focused coping mitigates the emotional reaction to stress while problem-focused strategies are used to manage and resolve the stressful situation (Folkman, Lazarus, Dunkel-Schetter, DeLonges, & Gruen, 1986; Folkman, Lazarus, Pimley, & Novacek, 1987; Lazarus & Folkman, 1984). Problem-focused coping strategies include confronting the problem, which involves risk taking or hostility. Seeking social support involves obtaining emotional and informational support from others. With accepting responsibility, persons acknowledge the role that they played in the stressful situation. Planful problem solving involves conscious efforts to alter the situation. In contrast, emotion-focused coping strategies are used to manage the emotional reactions to stress. Distancing strategies result in detachment from the situation or creating a positive outlook. Escape-avoidance strategies involve wishful thinking or behavioral efforts to avoid the stressful situation. Positive reappraisal involves personal growth and may have a religious tone.

In our study, coping strategies were assessed by an episodic, process-focused view of coping using open-ended questions. The respondent was asked to think of a situation that could be solved and another daily concern that could not be solved. Respondents identified the coping strategy used in each situation.

As expected, the predominant type of coping remained stable over the course of the 9 years of the study period. For the weighted index of problem-focused coping, Wave 5 survivors used primarily problem-focused coping at baseline ($M = 2.0$) and 18 months later at Wave 4 ($M = 2.7$). Wave 4 survivors also used predominately similar strategies at both time points ($M = 2.0$ and 2.7, respectively). At the initial interview, however, the proportion of respondents using problem-focused coping strategies was significantly higher in those only interviewed at Wave 1 (73.7%) than for Wave 4 (56.2%) and Wave 5 survivors (52.2%). At Wave 4, the proportion of respondents using problem-focused strategies was not significantly different for Wave 4 (69.6%) and Wave 5 survivors (60.9%).

Respondents used a variety of coping strategies when it was possible to solve a problem. The most frequently used strategy was planful problem solving, with approximately 30% of subjects using it. The least-used strategies were confronting the problem (< 5%), positive reappraisal (< 22%), and escape or avoidance (< 1%). There were some interesting differences among respondents. Among Wave 5 survivors, nearly 22% used positive reappraisal and distancing as the second most frequent types of coping strategies followed by seeking social support (17.4%), which also was popular among Wave 4 survivors (27.5%) and those interviewed only at baseline (31.6%). By Wave 4, nearly 31% of the respondents used problem-solving strategies and seeking social support most frequently.

When the situation was an enduring concern or worry, the most frequent coping strategy at Wave 1 was distancing for those only interviewed at baseline (42.4%) and Wave 4 survivors (30.5%), whereas it was escape avoidance for Wave 5 survivors (29.4%). However, Wave 5 survivors used a broader range of coping strategies with similar proportions of respondents using escape avoidance, problem solving, and positive reappraisal (18%).

At Wave 4, the pattern of strategies used changed. The most frequent strategies were distancing (28.5%) and seeking social support (25.2%) for Wave 4 survivors, whereas Wave 5 survivors continued to use a broader range of coping strategies with approximately 18% using distancing, self-control, seeking social support, and planful problem solving.

Whether the diversity of coping strategies of Wave 5 survivors reflects a greater repertoire of strategies or greater diversity in this subgroup cannot be determined. Whether the greater diversity of coping strategies contributed to the greater longevity of those living at the last interview is also uncertain.

There is beginning evidence that women may use different types of coping than men use. In the presence of pain or dependence in ADLs from arthritis, women mobilized different types of social support with similar stressors (Roberts, Dunkle, et al., 1994; Roberts, Matecjyck, & Anthony, 1996).

At Wave 1, men (58.7%) used significantly more problem-focused strategies than did women for situations that could be solved (34.2%; χ^2 (df = 2) = 21.1, $p < 0.0001$). In contrast, women (33.6%) used positive appraisal more often than men did (8.7%; χ^2 (df = 2) = 11.7, $p < 0.003$). The weighted index of problem-focused coping revealed similar significant differences between men ($M = 2.0$) and women ($M = 2.8$, t [190] = −3.0, $p < 0.01$).

For continuing worries at the initial interview, men (28.2%) used significantly more problem-solving strategies than women did (7.8%; χ^2 (df = 2) = 18.4, $p < 0.01$). Compared with women, men used less escape avoidance (12.8%; χ^2 (df = 2) = 4.2, $p > 0.05$), whereas women (20.2%) used more positive reappraisal than men did (2.6%; χ^2 (df = 2) = 24.2, $p < 0.001$). Because the referent problem the respondent used was not elicited, it is possible that women reflected about a very different problem than did men. What accounts for this gender difference in coping style is not clear and requires further research.

No information regarding the situations selected was obtained. Because the type of situation may have affected the coping strategies, the measurement of these strategies may be affected by unknown biases. As with stressful life events and worry, the accuracy of recall is also an issue in the measurement of coping. A weighted index of coping was constructed with a range of 0 to 6, with lower scores indicating greater use of problem-focused strategies. Although the index of coping provides a summary of the type of strategies used, the frequency of specific strategies is not revealed. (See the Appendix for a more complete description of the measurement strategy for coping.)

Self-Esteem and Mastery

Although low self-esteem is related to greater depression (Krause, 1987b; Pearlin et al., 1981), its contribution to the amelioration of stress is not well-known (Roberts, Dunkle, et al., 1994), although some evidence exists that it does (Rodin, 1989). At Wave 1, self-esteem was negligibly related to positive and negative life events ($r < 0.08$). However, greater self-esteem was significantly related to less worry ($r = -0.22$, $p < 0.01$).

Another context by which the oldest-old may evaluate their life circumstances is mastery. This resource reflects the ability of persons to control circumstances and ongoing events and their ability to manage them effectively (Pearlin et al., 1981). Mastery sets the expectation about one's competence in meeting the daily challenges of life. Unlike younger cohorts, mastery is multidimensional in nature for the very old (see Appendix) (Roberts, Dunkle, & Haug, 1994) and has been related to better mental health (Turner & Noh, 1988).

At the initial interview, global control, an aspect of mastery, was not significantly related to positive or negative life events ($r = -0.06$) but was significantly associated with less worry ($r = -0.33$, $p < 0.01$). In contrast, perceived control of events, another aspect of mastery, was significantly related to lower worry ($r = -0.20$) but not positive or negative events ($r = -0.08$). These findings suggest that the two dimensions of mastery are more important to worry than are life events. Because worry reflects the daily challenges of life, confidence in one's ability to manage these may affect one's interpretation of them as stressful as well as the expectations of the effectiveness of coping strategies used.

Social Support

Social support is a coping resource that has received significant attention in reducing the effects of stress. It is the interaction between people and has most frequently been conceptualized as the provision of tangible and intangible benefits (Blazer, 1982). Interactions with others are a requisite for social support (Fillenbaum, 1988). Although others may be available to provide support, the very old must be willing and able to interact with others. Many family and friends of the very old have died, reducing the size of the social network available to provide support (Field & Minkler, 1989).

The size of the social network reflects the potential for support that may be available to the very old. To be a resource, contacts with and help from members of the social network must be available in times of need (Fillenbaum, 1988; Roberts, Anthony, et al., 1994; Roberts, Dunkle, et al., 1994). Yet, the older adult may identify persons as part of their social network but have very little contact with them. For example, friends or family members may be unable to interact because of disability, illness, or geographic distance. An older adult with a small network who interacts frequently may receive significantly more social support compared with a person with a larger social network but few interactions with it.

At the initial interview, positive life events were significantly associated with a larger social network ($r = 0.15$, $p < 0.05$), whereas the associations with negative life events and worry were not significant ($r = -0.10$ and -0.11, respectively). At Wave 1, negative life events were significantly associated with a lower frequency of social interaction ($r = -0.13$, $p < 0.05$), whereas the associations with positive life events and worry were not significant ($r = 0.05$ and -0.08, respectively). These findings must be interpreted with caution because the social resources mobilized with specific life events and worry were not determined.

Among community-dwelling elders, men and women mobilized social support differently in response to stress related to impaired mobility and difficulty in the performance of ADL and household IADLs (Roberts, Anthony, et al., 1994; Roberts et al., 1996). Women with greater impaired mobility used greater tangible support and emotional support, whereas men used very little tangible and emotional support in this circumstance.

For both men and women, the association of ADLs to negative life events and worry were small and not significant ($r < 0.16$). Using the r to z transformation to assess significance of differences in correlations (Kirk, 1982), the association between positive life events and ADLs was significantly larger for men than it was for women

($r = 0.28$ and 0.13, respectively; $p < 0.001$). In contrast, the association of IADLs to worry was significantly larger in women ($r = -0.22$) than it was in men (-0.15, $p < 0.001$), whereas the associations with positive and negative life events were small and not significant ($r < -0.11$).

Although specific types of social support used with specific stressors were not determined, these findings suggest that social support is an important resource in dealing with stress. Social support is mobilized with some types of stress, and men and women mobilize social support differently.

TRANSACTION MODELS OF STRESS

Moderating and mediating models of stress are transactional models and have been the focus of a great deal of research. These models depict the transaction between the person and environment, but the way in which personal resources mitigate the adverse effects of stress is different in each. In the moderating model, personal resources attenuate the relationship between stress and mental health (Wheaton, 1984). In the mediating model, stress mobilizes personal resources that directly affect mental health (Wheaton, 1984), and stress has an indirect effect on health through its influence on personal resources. Support for both models has been inconsistent and has varied depending on the stressful event or situation (George, 1989). As in most research of stress and coping resources, few studies have included the oldest-old, and fewer still have examined the role of stress and coping resources on mental health in the very old.

Psychological resources provide the context to evaluate the stressfulness of situations. Self-esteem reflects the person's sense of worth and may be used to appraise the degree of threat a potentially stressful situation may engender. Hence, self-esteem also can influence the perceptions of possibly stressful situations or conditions (Roberts, Dunkle, et al., 1994). Self-esteem has been found to have mediating effects on mental health (Penninx et al., 1997) and is associated with lower depression (Krause, 1987c; Pearlin et al., 1981). However, the moderating effects of self-esteem between the challenges of life and mental health have not been demonstrated (Roberts, Dunkle, et al., 1994).

Another psychological resource is mastery, which reflects the perceived ability to control situations and to manage them (Blaney, 1985; Pearlin et al., 1981; Pearlin & Schooler, 1978). Persons with a strong sense of mastery manage stressful situations and have been better able to deal with the challenges of life than do those with low mastery (Krause, 1987a; Roberts, Dunkle, et al., 1994). Mastery has been found to have both mediating (Penninx et al., 1997) and moderating effects (Pearlin et al., 1981; Penninx et al., 1997; Roberts, Dunkle, et al., 1994) on mental health.

Social support has been the focus of a tremendous amount of research, and its effects on mental health during stress have been of significant interest. Two aspects of support have been delineated. Enacted social support refers to the qualitative aspects of support, such as support actually received from others. The size of the social network reflects the structural characteristics of support.

Although the benefits of social support have been assumed, more recent work suggests that social support can have negative and positive effects (Finch & Zautra, 1992; Ingersoll-Dayton et al., 1997; Rook, 1994). How and when to mobilize social support and its interaction with other personal resources have not been delineated (Costa & McCrae, 1993). The size of the social network has not been associated with greater mental health (Antonucci, Fuhrer, & Dartigues, 1997; George, Blazer, Hughes, & Fowler, 1989; Oxman, Berkman, Kasl, Freeman, & Barret, 1992). In some studies, enacted social support has a direct and positive effect on mental health (Antonucci et al., 1997; Bienenfeld et al., 1997; Dimond, Lund, & Caserta, 1987; George, 1989; George et al., 1989; Oxman et al., 1992), whereas, in other cases, this has not been found (Ormel et al., 1997). Similarly, the moderating effects of social support on the relationship between stress and mental health have not been found consistently (Holahan & Holahan, 1987; Krause & Markides, 1990; Penninx et al., 1997; Revicki & Mitchell, 1990; Roberts, Dunkle, et al., 1994).

Although health and functional abilities have been associated with mental health, few have considered that this is a physical resource that can be used to respond to stress. These resources may be more important in the very old, who experience failing health and declining independence in the performance of daily activities. If a great deal of time is needed to perform daily activities, little time and physical resources may be available to manage other stressful situations. Many have demonstrated that poor health is associated with poor mental health (Kathol & Petty, 1981; Ormel et al., 1997) and disability (Ormel et al., 1997; Turner & Noh, 1988). In contrast, the moderating effects of disability have not been demonstrated in some studies (Penninx et al., 1997) but found in others (Roberts, Dunkle, et al., 1994).

Coping strategies are behavioral and cognitive efforts to manage the challenges of life. That is, coping is goal oriented. These strategies can modulate the emotional reaction to stress or manage the stressful encounter (Folkman et al., 1986; Lazarus & Folkman, 1984).

Using data from Wave 1 and Wave 4, the mediator and moderator models of stress were evaluated. The effects of stress were examined in the presence of psychological (mastery, self-esteem), social support (frequency of social interaction), and physical resources (perceived health, ADLs, and IADLs) on general mental health (perceived health and general mental health assessed by the Bradburn Affect Balance Scale) and depression. Because IADLs and ADLs were highly related ($r = 0.87$), only IADLs were used because this variable had more variability than ADLs had.

Mediator Model

Multiple regression was used to assess the mediator model, in which stress mobilizes personal resources, and these resources then affect mental health. Separate regressions for each of the seven personal resources at Wave 2 (frequency of social interaction, self-esteem, global mastery, control of events, perceived physical health, problem-focused coping, and IADLs) were regressed on stress at Wave 1. Separate regressions were used for each measure of stress (worry and positive and negative life events) as an independent variable, and depression, rating of mental health, and general mental health as dependent variable. In another set of regressions, Wave 2 personal resources were regressed on mental health at Wave 4 using the appropriate Wave 1 mental health as a control variable. This analysis maximized the information about change inherent in this longitudinal study and allowed for assessment of temporal causal effects. (See

Table 5.3 for a summary of the effects of personal resources on mental health.)

Stressful Life Events

Stress explained a significant amount of variance in personal resources, ranging from 5% for frequency of social interaction to 16% for global mastery. Except for problem-focused coping and IADL, worry was a significant predictor of Wave 2 personal resources: self-esteem, rating of physical health, global mastery, and control of events ($\beta > 0.30$). Except for problem-focused coping, IADL and frequency of social interaction, positive life events at Wave 1 were

TABLE 5.3 Mediating Model: Effects of Personal Resources on Mental Health While Controlling for Wave 1 Mental Health

Variable	Depression		Bradburn Affect Balance		Rating of Mental Health	
	Beta	Change in R^2	Beta	Change in R^2	Beta	Change in R^2
Wave 1 Mental Health		0.42*		0.34*		0.17*
Depression	0.55**		NA†		NA	
Bradburn affect balance			0.42*		NA	
Rating of mental health	NA		NA		0.30*	
Wave 2 Personal Resources		0.06		0.12**		0.09***
Frequency of social interaction	0.02		0.10		−0.06	
Self-esteem	0.04		0.02		−0.03	
ADL	−0.08		0.04		0.11	
Rating of physical health	−0.13		0.20***		0.21***	
Problem-focused coping	−0.11		−0.01		0.10	
Mastery						
Global mastery	−0.06		0.21**		0.13	
Control of events	−0.11		−0.03		−0.01	

†Not applicable to regression model
*$p < 0.001$
**$p < 0.01$
***$p < 0.05$

not significant predictors of any personal resource, and negative life events were a significant predictor only for frequency of social interaction ($\beta = 0.18$).

After controlling for Wave 1 general mental health, personal resources explained a significant amount of variance in general mental health at Wave 4 (12%) and rating of mental health (30%), but not depression. For each type of mental health, rating of physical health was a significant predictor, whereas global mastery was a significant predictor of general mental health (see Table 5.3 for a summary).

These findings support the ascertains of others (Krause & Jay, 1991) that specific types of stress are associated with different types of coping resources and add to the inconsistent results for the mediator model of stress. The influence of worry and life events on personal resources was different, with worry having greater effects on these resources.

Although others hypothesized that stress mobilizes coping (Lazarus & Folkman, 1984), problem-focused coping was not mobilized in the presence of worry or life events among the oldest-old. These findings may be related to the measurement strategy. The amount of problem-focused strategies used was quantified but was not associated with a coping strategy for a particular stressor. No attempt was made to determine how past experiences affected the selection of coping used, but these experiences have been important in the strategy used and the outcomes of stress (Aldwin et al., 1996). However, the lack of support for the mediator model may be related to the nonspecific measures of coping and the measurement of the amount of challenging life situations instead of stress experienced with specific events.

Stress influenced subsequent ratings of physical health but not ADLs. Perhaps disruptions in physical health were not great enough to be associated with dependence in performing daily activities. Surprisingly, ratings of health, but not independence in activities of daily living, did not significantly reduce depression but did improve general mental health. However, these very old respondents perceived themselves as primarily healthy, and the variation in ratings of health and ADLs may not have been great enough to explain mental health and depression.

Worry

In contrast to life events, worry mobilized self-esteem, providing a context to evaluate the degree of threat of a stressful situation and perhaps the confidence needed to deal with it. Unlike the findings of others (Penninx et al., 1997), self-esteem did not significantly improve mental health or decrease depression among the oldest-old. The effectiveness of self-esteem in coping with the challenges of life may be different between the oldest-old and the younger adults studied by others (Penninx et al., 1997).

Greater worry, but not life events, was related to lower mastery and is consistent with the findings of others (Penninx et al., 1997). The ongoing nature of worry may reflect the inability to adequately manage these situations. These ineffective experiences may reduce the confidence that the very old have in dealing with these ongoing life challenges. In contrast, life events are time limited and, hence, resolve with time. Thus, the very old may perceive that their abilities to manage these events have not changed.

Social Support

Social support has been seen to improve mental health (Antonucci et al., 1997; Bienenfeld et al., 1997; Dimond et al., 1987; George et al., 1989; Oxman et al., 1992), but this was not the case in this study. Different types of social support are mobilized with different specific stresses (Roberts, Anthony, et al., 1994; Roberts et al., 1996). However, the frequency of social interaction measured in these very old respondents did not capture specific types of social support used. Moreover, social interaction may not have been associated with the provision of support and may explain its nonsignificant effects on depression and mental health.

Moderator Model

For the moderator model, the effects of personal resources were expected to attenuate the relationship between stress and mental health. Depression, rating of mental health, and general mental health as measured by the Bradburn Affect Balance Scale at Wave 4 were used as dependent variables in this analysis. Hierarchical multiple regression was used to identify the personal resources that had significant main effects on mental health—an assumption of a moderator model (Aiken & West, 1991). To control for previous mental health, Wave 1 mental health was entered at the first step and followed by stress and personal resources. To maximize the ratio between subjects and independent variables in the regression, two separate regressions were computed for worry and life events. Multiplicative terms were computed between stress and each significant main effect and were added after all significant main effects. To reduce multicolinearity between main effects and interaction terms, the variables were centered (Aiken & West, 1991). That is, the mean of a variable was subtracted from the score. Since centering does not affect unstandardized regression coefficients (Aiken & West, 1991), only these coefficients are reported. Table 5.4 is a summary of the unstandardized regression coefficients of interaction effects. To assess the nature of the interaction effects, the regression coefficients for stress at low and high levels of the moderator (one standard deviation [SD] below and above the mean) were determined (Aiken & West, 1991). (See Table 5.4 and Figures 5.1 through 5.3 for a summary of findings.)

The effects of positive life events on any type of mental health were not significantly altered by any personal resource. Hence, the moderator model for positive life events was not supported in our study. Since none of the main effects for personal resources were significant for ratings of mental health, the moderator model of stress for ratings of mental health was also not supported in our study.

General Mental Health

For general mental health, worry ($b = -0.56$, $p < 0.001$) was added, followed by IADLs, global mastery, and frequency of social interaction and accounted for 51% of the variance in this type of mental health. The addition of interaction terms explained only 2.4% more variance, and only the interaction term for global mastery was significant. The negative impact of worry on general mental health was highest for persons with low global mastery than it was for those for whom it was high.

TABLE 5.4   Unstandardized Regression Coefficients of Interaction Terms Between Stress and Personal Resources for Mental Health

Interaction	Unstandardized Regression Coefficients for Interaction	Change in R^2 for Interaction Effects
Depression[†]		
Worry with		0.02
Global mastery	0.01[*]	
Control of events	−0.27	
IADL	−0.16	
Problem-focused coping	0.08	
Bradburn Affect Balance[‡]		
Negative life events with		0.02
IADL	0.04[*]	
Global mastery	−0.05	
Frequency of social interaction	0.04	
Worry with		0.02
Global mastery	−0.95[*]	
Frequency of social interaction	0.09	
IADL	0.01	

[*]$p < .05$
[†]Controlling for Wave 1 depression
[‡]Controlling for Wave 1 Bradburn Affect Balance

For general mental health, negative life events ($b = -.038$, $p < 0.001$) were added, followed by IADL, global mastery, and frequency of social interaction, which accounted for 70% of the variance in mental health. The addition of the interaction terms explained only a small amount of variance, with only the interaction for IADL being significant. Greater independence in IADL was associated with lower mental health; greater independence was associated with greater mental health.

Depression

For depression, worry ($b = 2.12$, $p < 0.001$) was added followed by IADLs, global mastery, control of events, and problem-focused coping that explained 62% of the variance in depression. Only the interaction term for global mastery was significant, and a high level

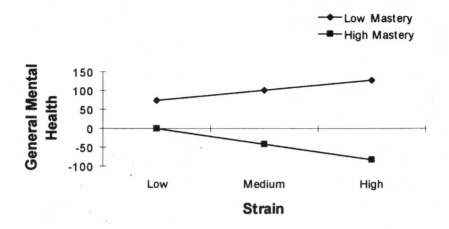

FIGURE 5.1   Attenuating effects of global mastery on the relationship between general mental health and strain.

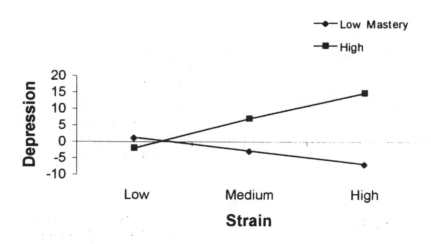

FIGURE 5.2   Attenuating effects of global mastery on the relationship between depression and strain.

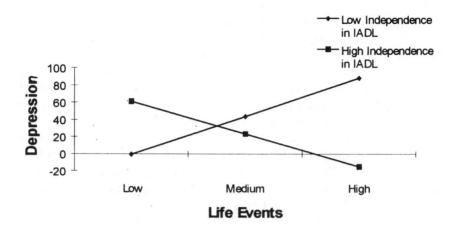

FIGURE 5.3 Attenuating effects of IADL on the relationship of negative life events and depression.

of global mastery was associated with greater depression; low levels were associated with lower depression.

These findings provide limited support for the moderator model of the effects of stress on mental health. Social support did not attenuate the effects of worry or life events. Because many of the very old respondents experienced recent deaths and illness of significant others, their social network may have been reduced or unable to provide the support that they needed. However, only frequency of social interaction was measured, and this does not reflect enacted support that is essential in dealing with these stressful situations. These findings add to the inconsistent support for the moderating effects of social support (Holahan & Holahan, 1987; Krause & Markides, 1990; Penninx et al., 1997; Revicki & Mitchell, 1990; Roberts, Dunkle, et al., 1994).

Although ratings of physical health did not attenuate the effects of stress, independence in IADLs did moderate the effects of negative life events, but not worry, on general mental health. These findings are inconsistent with others who found that IADL attenuated the effects of worry on general mental health (Roberts, Dunkle, et al., 1994). However, previous investigators used cross-sectional data that did not capture the change over time used in our longitudinal study. Because independence in these activities may reflect good health and physical abilities to perform them, a very old respondent with little or no disability may be better able physically to meet the challenges associated with time-limited negative life events. In contrast, better physical health and independence in ADLs may have already attenuated the chronic nature of worry that may have been present for a long time, and no more change may be possible.

Problem-focused coping did not attenuate the effects of stress on mental health among these very old respondents. As for the mediator model of stress, the measurement of coping did not capture specific coping strategies used with specific types of stress but reflected the amount of problem-focused strategies generally used. This lack of specificity may account for the lack of support for either model of stress.

Interestingly, mastery did not attenuate the effects of stress on mental health as was found by others (Pearlin et al., 1981; Penninx et al., 1997; Roberts, Dunkle, et al., 1994). Unlike younger age groups, mastery was multidimensional among the very old, and these findings provide new insight into the moderating effects of mastery. Global mastery magnified the effects of worry on depression and the adverse effects on general mental health; control of events did not have any significant moderating effects. Poor health and dependence in ADLs may adversely affect the control that the very old have over their everyday circumstances. Although the very old respondents may have believed that they had control over events, this perception may not have been consistent with reality. Frequent and prolonged inability to meet their expectations about their abilities may have led to disappointment and had an adverse impact on mental health. Those with perceptions of greater mastery may have been at a greater risk and failed to deal successfully with stressful situations.

SUMMARY

Evidence for the mediator and moderator models of stress has been inconsistent, and the findings of our study are no exception. Differences in measurement strategies and lack of specificity in linking a specific stressor to a specific personal resource may account for these inconsistencies. However, the nature of the stresses experienced by the very old may also explain the ineffectiveness of these personal resources. The most frequent life events experienced were death of a significant other and poor health of respondents and other family members and friends. Moreover, the most frequent worries experienced were poor physical health and factors that impaired mobility and the ability to perform daily activities. These worries were probably not new and may have already significantly influenced the very old respondents' perceptions of themselves and their abilities to meet these challenging situations. Neither the mediator nor the moderator model may adequately depict the nature of the transactions between the challenges of life, personal resources, and mental health. More longitudinal research is needed to determine the temporal order and nature of these transactions.

CHAPTER 6

Mortality and Function Among the Very Old

T he 20th century has been described as the century of survival (MacFadyen, 1990), with more men and women worldwide beginning to "outlive their lifespan," because of declining fertility rates and falling death rates. By the year 2000, the United States will have the oldest elderly population in the world, and by 2005 one in three elders will be at least 80 years of age.

This increasing life span casts an optimistic glow on growing old, until the lives of these very old people are examined more closely. Declining death rates come at the price of increasing health problems. There is evidence that declining mortality can lead to worsening health. Although overall mortality has declined, there is evidence of worsening health in the surviving population (Olshansky, Rudberg, Carnes, Cassel, & Brody, 1991).

Issues of disability and function become a central concern for people as early as the age of 45, escalating with advancing age. Compared with children and younger adults, older people experience fewer acute conditions but greater restriction in activities associated with these conditions (National Center for Health Statistics [NCHS], 1984). In general, for all age groups, chronic diseases have superseded acute disease (Fries, 1980). Chronic diseases account for more than 80% of all deaths and cases of total disability (Upton, 1983), although this picture varies by gender. Whereas men are more likely to have fatal acute episodes, women suffer more from disabling chronic diseases (Rosenwaike, 1985).

In general, the relationship between demographic characteristics and disability is consistent (Guralnik & Simonsick, 1993). These authors find that "there is a steeply increasing prevalence of ADL disability with increasing age, and women generally show higher rates of disability than men beginning around age 75 years" (p. 4). Overall, older people experience far greater major activity limitations than do younger people, for example, 39% of older people faced these limitations, whereas only 19% of those middle aged and 2% of children had the same restrictions (NCHS, 1984). Older age predicts lower functioning and the decline accelerates among the very old (Palmore, Nowlin, & Wang, 1985).

Of course, some of these findings depend on how disability and dysfunction are defined. Further, these figures may not reflect the ability of all people. It is important to clarify disability in the community from that among those who are institutionalized. Community surveys only represent a portion of the total disability in the older population because of the exclusion of those in nursing homes. Given that nursing home rates rise dramatically with age, there is an underrepresentation of the very old in community samples, especially in older women, one in four of whom reside in a nursing home (NCHS, 1984).

In this chapter, function and mortality issues among the elderly and particularly the very old will be examined. Results of analyses that identify correlates of function and mortality will be discussed.

ISSUES IN FUNCTIONING

It is anticipated that 17% of the total U.S. population will be elderly by 2020 (Siegel & Taeuber, 1993). Those over the age of 85 have quadrupled since 1950 to 2.6 million, with 45% impaired in either the instrumental or the physical ADLs (Zarit, Johansson, & Berg, 1993).

Physical functioning and age are significantly correlated, with the greatest limitations among those over the age of 85 (Parker, Thorslund, & Lundberg, 1994). Ten percent of those people over

65 still living in the community needed help with one or more personal care activities. Only 5% of persons 65 to 69 received help, compared with 31% of those over the age of 85. Among the 22% of those ages 65 and over who receive help with shopping, housework, and meal preparation, 14% were 65 to 69 and 51% were in the very old group. Schneider and Guralnik (1990) go further to examine the percentage of men and women at home in the community who need the help of another person: 10% of men 65 to 74 years of age and 37% of men over 85, as compared with 9% and 13%, respectively, of women.

Although many people function well in very old age, at least one third have significant disabilities (Zarit, Johansson, & Malmberg, 1995). Clearly, the proportion of persons with some functional limitation increases after the age of 65 years, with the largest proportion occurring in the old category (Katz et al., 1983). Factors that account for this increase in functional limitations are age-related decline in physical resilience and reserve strength. Although a high correlation between advanced age and functional disability is well-documented for the oldest-old, a considerable variance in functional level exists between groups (Feller, 1983). One well known factor is race. Evidence demonstrates a black/white crossover in functional health. A recent study (Clark, Maddox, & Steinhauser, 1993) showed that although younger black elders were more likely to experience functional decline over a 6-year period, this was not true among very old blacks. Another significant factor that may be related to race is socioeconomic status (Palmore, Nowlin, & Wang, 1985). Better education and higher income probably allow people to gain access to resources that contribute to better functioning, in other words, food, shelter, and health care.

Functioning, though, is variable, especially among the very old. An examination of the oldest-old in Sweden showed three patterns of functioning: those with high functioning, those with only deficits in IADL, and those with multiple disabilities. Functional loss in the very old can also be regained. The World Health Organization (1981) cited results that identify a greater potential for rehabilitation and regaining function for people of advanced age. The potential for rehabilitation exists even when lower functioning is the result of an untreatable disease (Besdine, 1988). An active approach to preserving function with advanced age includes changes in the medical and institutional response to disability, as well as in the negative attitudes about normal functional changes associated with aging that even the elderly accept.

With a pattern of codisabilities viewed as normative among this oldest-old group (Zarit, Johansson, & Berg, 1993), some old people are more likely to die than others. Research findings support the fact that poorer functioning is highly correlated with death (Kovar, 1988; Koyano, Shibata, Haga, & Suyama, 1986; Parker, Thorslund, & Nordstrom, 1992), institutionalization (Ostwald, Snowdon, Rysavy, Keenan, & Kane, 1989; Thorlund, Norstrom, & Wernberg, 1991), and the use of formal care services (Tennstedt, Sullivan, McKinlay, & D'Agostino, 1990). This means there is a significant health-care expenditure among these very old people, especially during the last year of life for institutionalized elders. Approximately 28% of Medicare for all enrollees was expended for care during that terminal period (Lawton, Moss, & Glickman, 1990). Zarit et al. (1995) believe that "the continued growth in numbers of the oldest old will put increasing pressure on both health-care and long term care services. Given the high rates of functional and cognitive disabilities, care for the oldest old should be expected to be complex and costly" (p. 21).

When studying the oldest-old, only the survivors are included in the sample (Parker et al., 1994). Examining the disability of these people represents only a portion of the health and function continuum. Therefore, some groups may be overrepresented, as Bury and Holme (1991) found in their sample, in which former white-collar workers were overrepresented. There may also be fewer people with fatal diseases.

In order to understand the overall burden of disability among the oldest old, it is important to include people in all living conditions (Guralnik & Simonsick, 1993). The picture of functional limitation is even worse when nursing home residents are taken into consideration. Schneider and Guralnik (1990) concluded, "the majority of women (62%) and a substantial proportion of men (46%) aged 85 years and above either reside in nursing homes or need assistance to live at home" (p. 2336).

FACTORS CONTRIBUTING TO FUNCTIONAL ABILITY

Functional status and disability are major areas of assessment when evaluating care needs. Several domains of functioning are usually considered: physical, cognitive, emotional, sensory, and social (Guralnik & Simonsick, 1993). In addition to age, which is related to decline in performance, Seeman et al. (1994) found that lower income, higher education, relative weight and blood pressure, lower peak expiratory flow, and prevalent diabetes and physical and cognitive functioning had the greatest impact on disability. Research also links functional ability to gender, marital status, health status (Kaplan, 1992; Roos & Havens, 1991; Guralnik & Kaplan, 1989), social supports, and affective states (Kaplan, 1992). It is also influenced by previous behavior. Regular physical activity, moderate alcohol consumption, and moderate weight, as well as the index combining all three of these health practices, appear to contribute to higher functioning (Camacho, Strawbridge, Cohen, & Kaplan, 1993).

VARIATIONS IN FUNCTION

There is also evidence that plasticity exists in functioning, as Manton (1988) and Strawbridge, Kaplan, Camacho, and Cohen (1992) demonstrated. Not all survivors in longitudinal studies continued to decline. A significant proportion actually improved over time. The variation in functioning highlights the complex issues in attempting to define normal aging. Historically, gerontologists have considered those who were impaired in comparison to those who were not. This blunt distinction camouflages two dimensions of function: those who function unusually well and those who are disabled but not necessarily acutely ill (Garfein & Herzog, 1995; Verbrugge, 1990). Responding to the fact that many research findings have tended to interpret age-associated deficits as age determined, Rowe and Kahn (1987) believed that lifestyles, health, and psychosocial factors can explain deficits attributed to the normal aging process. Pathological studies eliminate human response that could be determined by disease, so the resultant findings "tend to create a gerontology of the usual" (Rowe & Kahn, 1987, p. 143). Failure to recognize the substantial variability within groups (Rowe, 1982; Shock et al., 1984) eliminates the potential for examining successful aging as apart from usual aging. Rowe and Kahn (1987) underscored the need to examine the role of psychosocial factors in health and disease in order to understand usual and successful aging.

Unfortunately, the capacity to understand successful aging or aging that involves disability has been hampered by methodological problems. Exceptional performance has not been addressed in the development of measures of health and function. Also, it has been noted that at times the domains of function cannot be distinguished. For example, are people unable to feed themselves because of physical or cognitive problems (Guralnik & Simonsick, 1993)? The heterogeneity of functional ability at older ages, as well as the changes in function (some get worse while others get better), increased the need to expand measurement to include assessment over a wider range of functional ability (Seeman et al., 1994). With the increasing heterogeneity in functioning, this is an issue associated with increasing age (Suzman et al., 1992) and the increasing numbers of those who are over the age of 85 that needs to be addressed (Bould, Sanborn, & Reif, 1989; Taeuber & Rosenwaike, 1992).

MORTALITY

A large portion of deaths in developed countries occur after the age of 80; about one half of the female and one third of the male deaths (United Nations, 1991). Whether this is influenced by natural life expectancy (Harman, 1991; Carnes & Olshansky, 1993; Olshansky & Carnes, 1994) or by practical impediments (Olshansky, Carnes, & Cassell, 1990) that could be changed, most believe that death rates can only be affected by slowing the aging process. Increasing evidence exists that species do not have specific life span limits and that aging can be influenced by health interventions, environmental improvements, and behavioral changes (Kanniston, Thatcher, & Vaupel, 1994; Manton, Stallard, & Tolley, 1991), supporting the notion that mortality among the oldest-old could be reduced.

Mortality rates have been declining over a recent 35-year period. Kaplan (1992) demonstrated that from 1950 to 1986 mortality rates declined for people in the 65 to 74 year age group. The decline was even more substantial (24%) for those over 85. The result of the decline in mortality in old age has been due to greater morbidity and disability in older people (Crimmins, Saito, & Ingegneri, 1989; Rice & LaPlante, 1988; Rogers & Belanger, 1989). Olshansky et al. (1991) suggest two mechanisms to explain this phenomenon: medical management that has allowed people to live longer with diseases and a possible shift in the causes of disability that puts less emphasis on fatal diseases. More recently, projections continued to suggest that a decline in mortality rates and an increase in life expectancy (Guralnik, 1991) will exist for the next 50 years.

With the substantial increase in people over 85, it is anticipated that most of the disability in the 3 years prior to death will occur among those in this age group. In fact, Guralnik (1991) suggests that the years spent with chronic disease and disabilities may be increasing because comorbidity increases with age (Guralnik, La-Croix, Everett, & Kovar, 1989). Causes of disability probably include dementing illness, arthritis, and comorbid conditions, all of which are likely to increase with age. It is unclear what the implication is for the compression of morbidity if life expectancy continues to increase.

Certain factors seem to be related to morbidity. Schoenlfeld, Malmrose, Blazer, Gold, and Seeman (1994) found that poorer self-rated health was predictive of hospital and nursing home use and that this was true even when examining high-functioning elders. These authors suggest that health-care professionals should be sensitive to these issues when a seemingly well elder reports poor health.

Chipperfield (1993) also found a relationship between self-rated health and survival. Those who overestimate their health were less likely to die than those who did not. Overestimation of self-rated health did not seem to have a negative effect, and in fact "positive illusion enhances survival, even among those with grim future prospects." Other authors also support this incongruence between self-rated health and medically evaluated health. Kaplan, Barell, and Lusky (1988) review literature that supports the fact that the individual's self-evaluation is often incongruent with that of a medical examination. Although these ratings do seem to converge over time, the individual's evaluations of himself or herself are more predictive of the medical evaluation (Maddox & Douglas, 1973). Kaplan et al. (1988) also suggest that self-rated health may predict physical health more accurately.

Others have found a strong relationship between self-rated health and survival (Mossey & Shapiro, 1982), suggesting that it is not just a statement influenced by mood. Kaplan et al. (1988) state "What people feel or perceive about their health is meaningful; it influences behavior and adds information beyond other dimensions of health measures. The self-rating of health is an important psychosocial parameter in the evaluation of health status, in determining the prognosis of the elderly, and in analyzing survival" (p. 119).

THEORETICAL VIEW

One theoretical model that sheds some light on function and mortality is Selye's (1956) physiological model of stress reaction that was later modified by Lazarus and Laumier (1978). This model attempts to establish a causal link between stressful life events and health.

The effects of stress in producing illness have frequently been studied in social science and health since the mid-1960s (Holmes & Rahe, 1967), based on the assumption that older people are particularly vulnerable to the adverse effects of stress (Aldwin, 1996). Although this assumption was supported in early work (Holmes & Rahe, 1967), other studies have produced mixed results (Holahan, Holahan, & Belk, 1984). A more recent study found that older individuals were less likely than younger ones were to report a negative effect of stress on their health (Silverman, Eichler, & Williams, 1987).

Researchers have almost completely ignored the effects of stress on disability or functional impairment, a health condition that may be related to but is conceptually distinct from illness (Ford et al., 1988). This lack of knowledge is particularly problematic for the very old, those over the age of 85, whose increasing numbers include a large number of people suffering from functional limitations. It is not known whether the stress that very old people experience actually affects their functioning. If it does, then it is important to explore ways to moderate the relationship between stress and function. What resources come into play in the relationship between stress and function for this age group are also not known. The failing health and dwindling social resources of the very old may reduce the physical, psychological, and social assets available to them to meet the challenges of life. Given the diminished resources, the ability of these people to cope with the effects of stress may be reduced, placing them at greater risk for poor physical and instrumental functioning and death.

SOCIAL AND PERSONAL RESOURCES

The impact of stress on the older person's health is affected by a variety of factors, but social support, coping, and mastery are most important (Krause, 1987c). A sense of mastery offers a feeling of control over events in life that may be an important coping resource for older persons (Blaney, 1985). Persons with this sense of control manage stress more effectively than do those who feel that life is a matter of luck (Krause, 1987). For example, mastery has been found to attenuate the effects of strain on the mental health of the very old (Roberts, Dunkle, et al., 1994).

Initial research on social support focused on understanding why it was helpful to people who were coping with stress (Hobfoll, 1988); recent findings show modest effects in both helpful and harmful ways (Sarason, Sarason, & Pierce, 1990). Social support is conceptualized as interaction with a social network; persons in this network assist the individual to manage the problems of life. Persons with strong personal resources have greater access to supportive networks and use the networks more effectively than do those with weaker personal resources (Caldwell & Reinhart, 1988).

Social support may also affect the ability of the individual to perform the ADLs. Unfortunately, among the very old, the size of the network may diminish as friends and relatives die, and the ability to provide support may decline as health deteriorates. However, social support has not been found to attenuate the effects of life events and strain on mental health among the very old (Roberts, Dunkle, et al., 1994). It remains unclear how social support interacts with personal and environmental resources (Costa & McCrae, 1993) to affect the functioning of the very old.

Because the general condition of the very old has been reported chiefly through cross-sectional data, what accounts for change in function over time or indeed whether events cause change in function or vice versa is unknown (Murrell, Norris, & Grote, 1987). The research presented examines, over a 9-year period, the relationship of stress to decline in function and death, taking into account social and personal factors that moderate this relationship among very old adults.

In summary, little is known about the relationship between stress and functional capacity and mortality among people age 85 and over. Furthermore, the variability of functional levels in relation to mortality is little understood. Existing knowledge of the very old is limited, and largely negative, such as statistics on various chronic diseases and mortality, or largely speculative, such as views about the impact of losses or stressful life events. What stresses and worries people in this age group experience, what factors promote functional ability, and what relationships exist between stress and functional ability and mortality remain open for investigation.

METHODS (See chapter 2)

Measurement

Two aspects of functioning were examined: physical and instrumental ADLs. The Katz Activities of Daily Living Index (Katz, Ford, Moskowitz, Jackson, & Jaffee, 1963) was used to assess physical functioning. This index measures the respondent's ability to perform six ADL: feeding, getting in and out of bed, bathing, dressing, walking, and taking care of one's appearance.

IADL measured by several items from the Older Americans Resources and Services (OARS) assessment relating to using the telephone, shopping, taking medication, preparing meals, going places, doing housework, and managing finances. The range of scores was 0, needing help with everything, to 14, needing no help.

A modified version of the Hassles Scale (Kanner et al., 1981) was used to determine the most common everyday strains experienced by the very old.

Closed-ended questions were used to measure coping resources that were related to the individual's personality. Personal resources included a sense of mastery and self-esteem. Mastery over events was measured by a seven-item Likert scale developed by Pearlin and Schooler (1978). These items were statements about a person's ability to control events, and the respondents indicated the degree to which they thought the item described them or not. In this analysis, two factors were used: global mastery and perceived control (see Chapter 2 for greater description). Rosenberg's (1965) Self-Esteem Scale measured global self-esteem. The scale consisted of five descriptive items scored on the Guttman Scale that the respondent rated as applicable to him or her.

Conditional attributes viewed as resources include social support, health status, and mental health measures of depression and well-being. The eight items of the subscale, Social Resources, from the OARS instrument were used to assess social support. The respondent rated the frequency of support offered.

Health status was measured using several measures: self-reported health, number of hospital days and number of sick days in the last 6 months, and ADL.

Two measures of mental health were included. The Bradburn Affect Balance Scale was used as a measure of well-being. The negative and positive subscales were combined for a score that ranged from 1 to 5, low to high. Socioeconomic status of each elder was ascertained using the Hollingshead Two Factor Scale.

Depression was measured using the six-item depression subscale of the Derogatis SCL-90 Scale (Derogatis, 1977). The questions concerned whether he or she was hopeless about the future, had thoughts of ending his or her life, had thoughts of worthlessness, had nervousness inside, felt fearful, or felt tense. (For more detail regarding measures please see the Appendix.)

Analyses: Descriptive Analyses and Multiple Regression Analyses

Descriptive statistics will be used to characterize all variables used in these analyses. The multiple regression analyses examined predictors of physical and instrumental ADL at the beginning of the study (Wave 1) and over the 9 years of the study (Wave 1 to Wave 5) using the same variables as the survival analysis. The survival analysis focused on identifying what variables, including functioning, had an impact on survival among this very old group of people. Stress was measured only by the Hassle Scale (worry) because the literature and our preliminary analyses indicated that the discrete measures of stress were unrelated to function.

Descriptive Results (see chapter 2 for a more detailed description)

Overall, respondents at Wave 1 report positive physical health and functioning, good social and personal resources, and good mental health. As shown in Table 6.1, at Wave 1, 77.7% of the respondents

TABLE 6.1   **Distribution of Categorical Variables**

	Wave 1	Wave 2	Wave 3	Wave 4	Wave 5
	N (%)	*N* (%)	*N* (%)	*N* (%)	*N* (%)
Sex					
Female	139 (77.7)	133 (80.1)	123 (80.4)	116 (81.1)	19 (90.5)
Male	40 (22.3)	33 (19.9)	30 (19.6)	27 (18.9)	2 (9.5)
Race					
White	148 (82.7)	140 (84.3)	127 (83.0)	119 (83.2)	17 (81.0)
Black	31 (17.3)	26 (15.7)	26 (17.0)	24 (16.8)	4 (19.0)
Living child					
Yes	120 (67.0)	112 (67.5)	103 (67.3)	98 (68.5)	16 (76.2)
No	59 (33.0)	54 (32.5)	50 (32.7)	45 (31.5)	5 (23.8)

were female, 82.7% were white, and 67% had a living child. Nine years later (Wave 5), 90.5% were female, 81% were white, and 76.2% had a living child. The mean age of the sample at Wave 1 was 87.7 years, with ages ranging between 84 and 98 years. In an effort to have adequate numbers to examine racial differences, blacks were oversampled, representing 17.6% of the total sample. The reported health and functioning of respondents at Wave 1 was positive. On average, respondents reported their health to be good and their functioning on ADL as high when the total ADL score was examined. The picture changed when the two separate measures of ADL were viewed, however. Although measures on physical ADL remained high over the 9-year study period, the decline was significant, the range was greater and the mean lower (10.13 out of a possible 12) at Wave 5. The mean score on functional ADL was 11.44 (SD = 0.92) on a scale with a range of 0 to 12, also indicating minimal dysfunction. By Wave 5 the mean on these measures for the survivors had declined to 10.1 (SD = 2.4) from 11.33 (SD = 0.97) at Wave 1. The picture was different for IADL. Although instrumental functioning remained high for the first 18 months of the study (Waves 1–4), there was a significant decline after that. At Wave 4 the IADL mean score was 11.54, but 7 years later, the mean score was 8.9, with a range from 3 to 14 on a 14-point scale. Self-rated health was high. Almost 61% of the sample felt that their health was good or excellent. Their average number of days spent sick or in the hospital were few in number at the beginning and end of the study but higher at Wave 4.

With regard to the respondents' social and personal resources, they possess a moderate sense of mastery and self-esteem at Wave 1. Interestingly, self-esteem improved by Wave 5 but mastery declined significantly. Social support was available to them, and they reported the frequency of that support as favorable. These two measures of support remained stable over the 9-year study period.

The mental health of respondents appeared to be good, as indicated by their report of a positive affect balance, little depression, and low stress due to worry at Wave 1. The most often reported worries over the last year at Wave 1 involved concerns about the health of a family member (48%). The remaining three most common worries in the last year involved concerns about falling (37%), about not having enough energy (32%), and about misplacing or losing things (29%). (See chapter 2 for a more extensive description.)

When examining worries by race, sex, and age, few differences emerge (results not shown). However, blacks are significantly more likely to note failing to take medication, to have concerns about money, and to worry more about neighborhood crime than whites are. Whites were more likely to worry about the health of a family member, having lessened physical abilities, and not having enough time. When considering sex differences in worries, results of a *t*-test examining mean differences showed that women experienced significantly more worry than did men.

By Wave 5 there was a significant increase in the number of worries these people had who were in their mid-90s. The following worries were at issue at least "a little bit" for the majority of survivors: health of a family member, weight, sleep, not enough energy, falling, fewer physical abilities, taking medication, increased forgetfulness, compromised mobility, health in general, physical appearance, too much time on hands, not enough time, difficulties with friends or family, money, regarding inner conflicts, troublesome neighbors, and neighborhood crime.

Predictors of Change in Function

The bivariate relationships between worry and ADL and IADL were significant, indicating that greater worry was related to poorer ADL and IADL functioning. Two regression equations (results not shown) examined the correlates predicating functional ADL and IADL at Wave 1. There was only one significant predictor of functional ADL, the factor from the mastery scale, "I can do just about anything I really set my mind to do." Worry was no longer significant after other measures were added. There were several significant predictors for instrumental activities; more frequent social interaction, greater perceived control, and less availability of social support predicted better ability to perform IADL. It should be mentioned that available support is a measure of people available to help with a range of tasks. Therefore, if people have less help available, it might mean that they had no need and therefore no one had been identified in these helping roles

The effects of social support and psychological resources and worry on decline in functional ability over the first 18 months of the study were examined. Factors that contributed significantly to decline in instrumental functioning at Wave 4 were the same measure at Wave 1, worry and depression. Factors that contributed significantly to instrumental functioning at Wave 4, such as worry, were the same measure at Wave 1. When examining factors that contributed to change in physical functioning over the first 18 months of the study, only greater physical functioning at Wave 1 made a significant contribution to better physical functioning 18 months later. It would have been ideal to conduct this analysis over the 9 years of the study and include Wave 5, but, unfortunately, the sample size of 23 at Wave 5 precluded this.

Factors Contributing to Survival

Methods of survival analysis were employed to analyze data in which some respondents were still alive at the time of analysis (right-censored data). The probability of death by age was estimated using the Kaplan-Meier estimator, and the hazard of death was modeled as a function of covariates using Cox regression.

Because respondents were enrolled at different ages and survival prior to enrollment could not be credited, survival analysis using left-truncated and right-censored failure times was required. Left-truncated Kaplan-Meier curves were calculated using SAS Proc Phreg with delayed entry. Cox regression was used to model the hazard as a function of several covariates simultaneously and, again, Proc Phreg with delayed entry was used.

The main purpose of this analysis was to investigate what factors contributed to the mortality of this very old group, how mortality was effected by sex and race of respondent, the presence of a living child, health and function, social and personal resources, and mental health. A respondent's health and ability to function were operationalized as self-reported health, ADL, number of hospital days, and number of sick days. Mastery, self-esteem, availability of social support, and quality of social support composed respondents' social and personal resources. Mental health factors consisted of depression, affect, balance, and worrying. All variables were entered initially and deleted in a step-down fashion. Decisions to drop variables from the model were based on theory, the size of the p-value, and the size of the risk ratio. A significance level of 0.10 was deemed acceptable because a small data set such as this one might result in marginally significant effects. However, if the risk ratio was much higher than 1.00 or much lower, the variable was not dropped regardless of the significance level.

All demographic variables (sex, race, and whether respondent had a living child) were modeled using baseline values. Recognizing that health changes could possibly affect mastery, self-esteem, availability of social support, quality of social support, affect balance, depression, and worry over time, these variables were also entered as time-dependent covariates. Furthermore, since the possibility of circular influence exists (i.e., poor health leads to low self-esteem), the analysis was simultaneously adjusted for time-dependent health measures, such as self-reported health, ADL, number of hospital days, and number of sick days. Death occurred in the 7-year interval between the fourth and fifth waves, so linear interpolation was used to impute values for the time-dependent covariates. For people who died between Wave 1 and Wave 4, data from the most recent wave were used (Table 6.2).

Of the 193 respondents, 14 were dropped from the analysis because of an inordinate amount of missing data. Various physical and mental health problems prevented these respondents from completing one or more interviews. Missing values were imputed for another 11 respondents using the average of the previous and next waves.

TABLE 6.2   Mean Values and Standard Deviations of Continuous Variables

	Wave 1		Wave 2		Wave 3		Wave 4		Wave 5	
	X	(SD)	X	(SD)	X	(SD)	X	(SD)	X	(SD)
Health and Function										
Self-reported health	1.77	(.80)	1.75	(.81)	1.63	(.77)	1.59	(.83)	1.62	(.74)
ADLs	23.36	(2.78)	23.08	(3.01)	23.24	(3.05)	23.07	(3.13)	19.71	(5.02)
Number of hospital days	.94	(3.72)	.63	(2.45)	1.45	(5.23)	1.36	(4.68)	.67	(2.20)
Number of sick days	.46	(.89)	.36	(.78)	.59	(.97)	.38	(.78)	.48	(1.03)
Social and Personal Resources										
Mastery	12.41	(3.50)	12.90	(3.26)	13.59	(3.83)	13.09	(3.96)	9.00	(4.15)
Self-esteem	11.66	(3.43)	11.36	(3.36)	11.43	(2.85)	11.22	(3.57)	13.24	(2.90)
Availability of social support	3.96	(1.10)	3.93	(1.16)	4.22	(.97)	4.13	(1.04)	4.10	(.94)
Quality of social support	9.60	(1.79)	9.96	(1.41)	9.99	(1.47)	9.45	(2.07)	9.48	(2.27)
Mental Health										
Affect balance	6.92	(2.07)	7.14	(2.11)	7.08	(2.08)	6.67	(2.02)	6.67	(2.11)
Depression	1.99	(2.73)	2.39	(3.08)	2.38	(3.17)	2.94	(3.69)	3.57	(4.28)
Worry	7.17	(6.48)	5.79	(6.32)	5.92	(5.00)	11.26	(9.34)	27.57	(6.74)

The resulting 179 respondents were entered into the analysis. Of these cases, 65 were censored because respondents could not be located for an interview at some point in the study.

Survival was examined over all five waves of data of the study. Initially, all categorical and continuous variables were placed in the model. Cox regression revealed many of these variables to be nonsignificant, and these were deleted one at a time from the model until all p-values were less than 0.10. The final model is presented in Table 6.3. Variables included in the model that significantly predict survival are sex of respondent, self-reported health, depression, and

TABLE 6.3 Cox Regression Output

	Parameter Estimate	Standard Error	Wald Chi-Square	Pr > Chi Square	Risk Ratio
Gender	0.741	0.21615	11.75614	0.0006	2.10*
Depression	0.1004	0.03126	10.31712	0.0013	1.106*
Worry	−0.054	0.01411	14.59019	0.0001	1.106*
Health	−0.248	0.13090	4.74251	0.0294	0.76**

*p 0.01
**p 0.10

worries. Cox regression output is included for these variables that have been shown to be related to a higher risk of death.

Race and having a living child were not significant factors in a respondent's risk of death; however, not surprisingly, sex of the respondent did play a role. As illustrated in Figure 6.1, female respondents lived longer than men of all ages. The risk ratio (2.10) reveals that at all ages men have more than twice the risk of death compared with women.

Self-reported physical health was the only health and functioning factor determined to be a significant risk factor for dying. The risk ratio for self-reported health (0.76) indicates that respondents reporting poorer health are at greater risk of death than are those reporting better health. A respondent's ability to perform his or her ADLs, as well as the number of sick days that interfered with his or her functioning and the number of days spent in a hospital, were not significant factors in a respondent's risk of death.

Of the three mental health factors included in the model, only depression and worry were found to be significant. The risk ratio for depression (1.106) indicates that the higher the respondent's level of depression, the greater their risk of death. The risk ratio for worry (0.948) indicates that it is also a significant factor in a respondent's risk of death. Respondents experiencing higher levels of worry have a lower risk of death. Well-being was not a significant factor in one's risk of death.

Interestingly, none of the social and personal resources was significant.

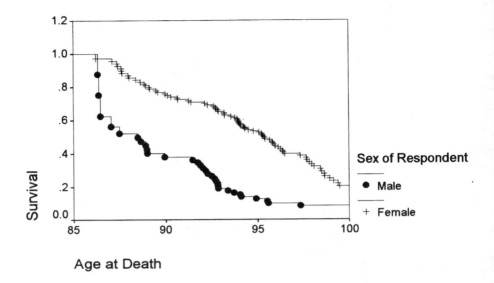

FIGURE 6.1 **Left truncated Kaplan Meier survival distribution for males and females.**

DISCUSSION

With so little known about the lives of the very old, it is important to understand what contributes to the functioning and mortality of these very old people. This chapter examined three aspects of their lives: what worries are experienced by people in this age group, what factors promote functional ability, and what relationship exists between worry and functional ability and mortality.

By and large, the group of very old people who were included in this study functioned very well. In large part, this was due to the fact that at the outset of the study, the convenience sample was identified while these subjects were residing in the community. Further, the most notable changes over the 9 years were in the measures of depression and worries, both increasing significantly.

After identifying aspects of the lives of these very old people and determining which ones had changed over the 9-year period, it was important then to determine what factors contributed to their functional ability. Worry, health, social and personal resources, and mental health were considered. Although the very old people in this sample experienced functional decline, a fact supported by Zarit et al. (1995) as well as Parker et al. (1994), there is variability even among these very old people. Therefore, it is important to identify factors that promote better function. These were examined for Wave 1 and then over the first four waves of the study (18 months). The mastery measure, reflecting the belief that the elder can do what he or she wants to do (perceived control), was the only variable at Wave 1 that was significantly related to ADL functioning at Wave 1, indicating that the person's ADL functioning was better when he or she had a greater sense of perceived control. Change in ADL functioning between Wave 1 and Wave 2 was predicted by ADL functioning at Wave 1. The worry had no significant bearing on ADL functioning at Wave 1 or change in ADL between Wave 1 and Wave 2.

IADL at Wave 1 had many more aspects of health and social and personal resources associated with them, for example, a greater sense of the aspect of mastery in which the elder feels he or she can do what he or she wants to do; less available social support; and higher frequency of social support. Although less available social support seems a peculiar association with increased IADL functioning, the social support measure reflects the availability of people to help. If the person's functional ability was higher, one would not expect to have an increased availability of people to help. None of the measures of mental health was significantly associated with IADL or ADL. In part, other gerontological researchers support these findings. Although we did not find health or affective measures related to function, as did Kaplan (1992), we found social support related to better instrumental functioning. In addition, the results of this study identified perceived control, a dimension of mastery, as a significant predictor of better ADL and IADL ability.

When examining factors that contributed to change in instrumental functioning over the first 18 months of the study, lower depression, better function, and increasing worry at Wave 1 made a significant contribution to better IADL 18 months later. Stress has a well-established relationship to health (Selye, 1956), but not so with functional ability. Our results, although connecting worry to better functioning, are unconventional, in that we found that increased worry is related to improved functioning in IADL. It is possible that worry is an indication that the older person is involved in the day to day activity of life with other people, and this connection promotes a positive relationship in instrumental abilities. We, as well as Kaplan (1992), also found lower depression related to better IADL functioning. The factors at Wave 1 that predicted death 9 years later were poorer self-reported health, being male, increased depression, and lower worry. Poorer self-reported health, greater depression, and being male are measures that have been found to predict mortality in many age groups. The surprising finding is that subjects who experienced a lower worry were more likely to die. This could be due to a lower sense of connectedness to the world around them. Many of the worries that the subjects identified had to do with connection to other people. Possibly the subjects who died were ones who lacked this sense of connection and who were possibly more depressed, as the significant correlation between worry and depression indicates. This idea was also supported in the earlier finding that increasing worry is associated with better IADL. Measures of function were not related to survival, nor were other health-related measures.

In part, the findings of the survival analysis in this sample of the very old are supported by findings of other studies. Mossey and Shapiro (1982), as well as Kaplan et al. (1988), found a relationship between better self-reported health and survival. Roos and Havens (1991) and Guralnik and Kaplan (1989) support the male gender connection to mortality as well. This study also found a connection between increasing depression and decreasing worry and mortality. Although the relationship of depression to mortality has been established, a relationship between declining worry and death has not been found. Actually, this relationship has to date produced the opposite results (Selye, 1956). In all likelihood, it is the measure of worry used in our study that may hold the key to the understanding of this relationship. Worry may be a mechanism for keeping those who are very old engaged in living and reduce mortality.

CHAPTER 7

Conclusion and Recommendations for Future Services

The maintenance of health and independence in daily living are the most critical issues for the oldest-old (Roberts, 1999). Being able to perform activities related to personal care (e.g., dressing and eating) and instrumental tasks related to caring for the home and outside activities (e.g., shopping and handling finances) is essential for independent living. However, disease and disability threaten this independence. Dependence in daily activities increases the need for services and informal assistance from family and friends (Hing & Bloom, 1990; Hirsch et al., 1991; Manton, 1988). Finding the needed services and paying for them are critical issues for most elders. Although formal social services and informal help from family and friends may allow dependent elders to remain in their homes (Dello Buono et al., 1999), targeted interventions to promote and maintain mobility and independence in ADLs are equally important (Roberts, 1999). When the very old are no longer able to live alone safely, institutionalization may be necessary, possibly contributing to further dependence in daily activities (Langer & Rodin, 1976). One consistent contributor to institutionalization has been hospitalization, which has consistently been found to contribute to a decline in independence in the performance of daily activities (Cullen et al., 1984; Gillick, Serrell, & Gillick, 1982; Landefeld, Palmer, Kowal, Kresevic, & Rosenblatt, 1990; McVey, Becker, & Saltz, 1989; Hirsch et al., 1991). Interventions targeted to reduce the probability of hospitalization are essential in minimizing dependence and reducing the cost of health care.

Research focusing on maintaining independence among elderly adults has promoted the development of several theoretical models. For example, the disablement model (Verbrugge, Lepkowski, & Konkol, 1991), the ecological model of functional health based on person-environment fit (Hogue, 1984), and the model of functional impairment/limitation (Johnson & Wolinsky, 1993). However, the difference in nomenclature and measurement strategies used in these theories makes interpreting the literature difficult (see Roberts [1999] for an extensive discussion of these theories and issues). Nagi's (1991) model of disability will be used in this chapter because of its conceptual clarity and widespread use. Disability will refer to the ability to perform daily activities, and functional limitations refer to system-level abilities at the level of the whole person, such as being able to reach a shelf, walk a block, or climb stairs (Nagi, 1991). Limitations in body systems related to anatomy, physiology, or psychology will be referred to as impairment (Nagi, 1991).

This chapter is organized into three sections. The first focuses on the living environments of the very old, another on formal services and the last on interventions targeted to impairments, functional limitations, and disability. Although other services and interventions are also relevant to the very old, only those directly related to maintaining independence in daily activities and supporting those who are dependent are discussed.

LIVING ENVIRONMENTS

A large proportion of the very old live alone, and those living alone may be healthier and less disabled than are those living in other settings (Bould et al., 1989). Although many elderly adults prefer to remain in their own homes, they can become isolated when functional limitations make leaving the house and seeking assistance from others difficult (Martin et al., 1996; Bureau of the Census, 1997). The availability of persons to provide help when needed is crucial to supporting the very old, who may need assistance to remain in their own homes (Fillenbaum, 1988), with family and friends critical to preventing institutionalization (Sanborn & Bould, 1989). The oldest-old often outlive their potential sources of social support from family and friends, but nearly 80% receive assistance from informal caregivers (Soldo & Myllyluoma, 1983). In our study, we found that relatives who were likely candidates to be caregivers died during the 9 years of the study. We found, however, that our respondents were able to maintain the availability of people to provide support as well as frequency of social contact.

The spouse is an essential provider of assistance for the married, and those who are widowed, single, or divorced are more likely to be institutionalized (Cohen, Tell, & Wallack, 1986). Yet, the very old often are women who have lost a spouse and must rely on others for assistance. This was also the case among our sample survivors. Findings from our study revealed that approximately 20% identified a child as being able to provide assistance whereas none identified a sibling. These individuals may also be in poor health and unable to provide care. In contrast, a younger child may have to choose between working and providing care.

When spouses and children are unable or unwilling to provide support, the very old may look toward their social network of friends and neighbors. In our study, nearly one third identified a friend and 13% identified a neighbor as being able to provide the most assistance. As with children, these individuals may be elderly themselves or have other significant work and family responsibilities that preclude their ability to provide assistance.

Although many of the very old may prefer assistance that allows them to remain in their own homes, the needs of the caregiver may preclude this. Hence, some of the oldest-old may move in with family and friends (Martin et al., 1996). The ability of these caregivers to provide assistance may depend not only on their own health but also on their time, abilities and desire to provide assistance. Often this living arrangement disrupts the lives of the caregivers and exhausts their resources. Although preventing institutionalization is desirable, it may be necessary when others are not available to provide assistance.

The match between the abilities of the very old and the supports in the environment are essential (Lawton & Nahemow, 1973; Lawton, 1982; Roberts & Algase, 1988). The very old can function to their maximum capabilities when the environment provides the context and supports consistent with their abilities. This is particularly true for the very old with cognitive and physical deficits. An environment that provides the environmental supports to assist the very old with mobility and safety features may allow them to function independently. Wheelchair accessible living quarters and access outside the home can support the very old whose mobility is severely impaired. Grab bars and raised toilet seats can be used in transfers; well-lighted living areas increase the safety of the very old with significant visual deficits. Reducing the environmental sensory information to the minimum required for assigning meaning to the environment makes it possible for the very old to understand their surroundings and respond appropriately (Hall, Gerdner, Zwycart-Stauffacher, & Buckwalter, 1995; Roberts & Algase, 1988).

Although the abilities of the very old should determine their living environment, the availability of willing and able persons in their social network to provide assistance when needed may preclude this. Institutionalization often results from lack of social support and not the decline in the physical and cognitive abilities of the very old. The lack of adequate social and financial resources may also preclude the very old from living independently in the community, necessitating the use of formal services.

FORMAL SERVICES

At times, formal services are not the sole resources but may provide an important adjunct to informal services. Formal services are those that are provided by organizations, and sometimes individuals, and may or may not require money to access them. Although there has been some concern that provision of formal services may reduce those provided by family and friends, this substitution effect has not been documented (Bould et al., 1988), and often the services are not used (Dello Buono et al., 1999). However, these services may provide much-needed assistance not available from others and also provide respite to caregivers.

Transportation services may be essential for the very old to go shopping and keep health care appointments, but they may not be easily accessible to the very old. Physical limitations may preclude the use of public transportation. Taxi services or owning a car may be too expensive for the very old on limited incomes. Although public transportation is available in urban areas, it is often not adequate or available in rural areas, and many of the very old in rural communities may have no access to affordable and reliable transportation. However, some communities and organizations provide door-to-door transportation for minimal or no cost.

Meal services may also be essential to maintain adequate nutrition. For homebound elderly adults, grocery shopping may not be possible, and food preparation may be difficult. Many organizations provide daily meal services with enough food to be used for more than one meal. Congregate meal services often abound in urban areas but require that the very old have reliable and safe transportation to get to these sites.

Many very old adults find it very difficult to do heavy housework and sometimes even the light cleaning necessary to provide a safe environment. Agencies and individuals may be able to provide home-maker chore services for a fee. Although this may be a hardship for some very old elders, others on limited incomes may qualify for assistance from Medicare and Medicaid that will pay for these services.

For the oldest-old dependent in personal care activities (e.g., bathing and dressing), daily home health aids may be required. Although many agencies can provide these services, some very old adults may purchase these services from unskilled persons. The elder may only need a little assistance in getting dressed and washing his or her feet and back, and unskilled persons are able to provide this assistance. Persons trained to provide basic personal care may be needed by the very old who require more assistance or by those who have difficulty getting in and out of bed or a chair. Often these services are only provided once a day. Those needing them more frequently may need to live with someone or to be placed in assistive living or extended care facilities.

Almost all of the very old have chronic illnesses and disabilities that require the ongoing services of skilled health professionals. Often these are nurses provided by home care agencies. Services may include monitoring blood pressure, dressing changes, and health lessons. Generally, a physician must prescribe home care services before third-party payers will cover these costs. Because hospital stays have been reduced with managed care, the need for home care services may be essential in allowing the oldest-old to remain in their own homes (Roberts, 1999).

Other community services may provide respite for caregivers of the very old. Respite services provide an opportunity for caregivers to be relieved of the burdens of care of the very old who are cognitively and physically impaired. Day care may allow caregivers to continue working or provide short respites from care. Hospice services provide support to the very old who are terminally ill and ensure a comfortable death.

The most effective services usually address the multiple underlying factors of disability. For example, outpatient geriatric assessment and management include services to determine the capabilities of the oldest-old and to implement interventions to reduce or compensate for deficiencies (Boult et al., 1994). During hospitalization, a complex set of nursing protocols can be implemented on an acute care unit for elders and used to focus assessment and intervention on common problems experienced in this population (Landefeld et al., 1990). A nurse-managed clinic can provide assessment and interventions to reduce functional limitations and disability (Boult et al., 1994; Evans, Yurkow, & Siegler, 1995), and nurses visiting older adults in their homes also can identify factors that contribute to increasing dependency (Robichaud, Hébert, Roy, & Roy, 2000). To be effective, the services should be multidisciplinary in nature and involve the elderly adult in planning. However, these multidimensional interventions are costly, with only small to modest effects. Hence, these services should be targeted to those most likely to benefit from the assessments, interventions, and services while minimizing their cost (time, personnel, and money) versus their benefits.

Coordinating formal services can be an overwhelming task for the very old and their caregivers. Time must be spent locating the needed services and coordinating them with the needs of the very old adult. Case managers, nurses, and social workers can be helpful in determining the services needed and then accessing them. They can coordinate formal services with those provided by family and friends. That is, they can tailor the services to meet the needs of the very old while supplementing their informal resources (Bould et al., 1988).

Some elders may pay for formal services, or they may be entitled to financial assistance from several federal and local programs. Medicare, Medicaid, Title XX of the Social Security Act, and Older Americans Act (Title III) pay for many formal services for those with limited financial resources. Private insurers may also pay for some services. Determining eligibility can be extremely confusing for the oldest-old and their caregivers, but case managers can provide help in navigating the intricate and complex eligibility requirements for these sources of funding.

INTERVENTIONS TARGETED TO IMPAIRMENTS, FUNCTIONAL LIMITATIONS, AND DISABILITY

All too often, elderly adults are treated as a homogeneous group contrary to the great heterogeneity in function among elders in this population related to aging, disease, history of physical activity, and life circumstances. The factors associated with functional limitation and disability will differ even among people with similar pathologies. The pattern of functional limitations and disability also may vary in different pathologies and impairments, which may require different interventions. For example, elderly adults with osteoarthritis in the knees as well as those with chronic heart failure may have functional limitations, such as inability to walk a mile or climb a flight of steps. Although the functional limitations are similar, the contributing underlying pathologies and impairments differ, and the appropriate interventions to reduce functional limitations may also differ. For example, a muscle strengthening and range of motion exercise program may strengthen the muscles surrounding the knee and increase range of motion of the knee while reducing pain. This exercise intervention may be most effective for the very old who have osteoarthritis (O'Reilly, Muir, & Doherty, 1999). Yet, this exercise program may have little effect for those with chronic heart failure when aerobic capacity and intrinsic changes in the muscle fibers of the lower extremities are responsible for these functional limitations.

For those with chronic heart failure, an aerobic exercise program may increase aerobic capacity and may be associated with some changes in the muscle fibers. Adding a strengthening exercise program may augment the changes in the muscle fibers associated with aerobic exercise.

Various functional limitations also may be associated with different types of disability (Roberts, 1999). The performance of IADLs is much more dependent on cognitive function than is the performance of ADLs, but functional limitations contribute to independence in both types of activities (Johnson & Wolinsky, 1993). For example, difficulty grasping and poor fine motor coordination of the hands make dressing and perhaps bathing and eating difficult. On the other hand, inability to get up from a chair may make toileting independently impossible, and impaired gait may contribute to difficulty in getting to the toilet or around the house and going shopping. Further, cognitive functional limitations, such as poor short-term memory or inability to follow instructions, would contribute to difficulty in managing money, shopping, or handling a medication regimen, all IADLs.

Data from our study of the oldest-old lend support to the fact that different functional limitations are related to different types of disability. Impaired gait, a functional limitation, was significantly related to greater dependence in ADL ($r = 0.55$) and IADL ($r = 0.62$). Toileting and transferring from chair and bed depend on safe gait, and those with impaired gait will probably need assistance from others to do these safely. The findings from our study add support to this. Although cognitive impairment was not significantly related to ADL ($r = 0.05$), it was associated with less independence in IADLs ($r = -0.33$).

Impairments

Although health care that is disease or illness specific is important, often overlooked are interventions that promote health and functioning and reduce disability. Interventions that contribute to independence are the focus of this section. First, those interventions specific to impairments of the upper extremities that have been found to be related to dependence in ADL (Lawrence & Jette, 1996;

Jette, Branch, & Berlin, 1990) will be addressed. Impairments of the lower extremity that have been found to be related to dependence in IADL will be mentioned (Lawrence & Jette, 1996). Special emphasis will be placed on balance, muscle strength, depression, and cognition because these were associated with independence in ADL (Cho et al., 1998; Ensrud et al., 1994; Rantanen, Guralnik, Sakari-Rantala, et al., 1999; Roberts, 1999). Even when interventions are not targeted to specific diseases, they have the potential to maintain or improve the ability of the oldest-old to live independently in the community.

Muscle Strength

Muscle strength of the lower extremities has been associated with limitations in arising from a chair, walking a known distance (Ades, Ballor, Ashikaga, Utton, & Nair, 1996; Kaufman, 1983; Fiatarone et al., 1990; Roberts, Wagner, Palmer, Mansour, & Srour, 1993), abnormalities in gait that contribute to falls (Rantanen, et al., 1999), and greater disability (Rantanen, et al., 1999). Inactivity, often found among the oldest-old, contributes to poor muscle strength (Bassey, 1998). A few days of inactivity reduce strength, with the postural control muscles being affected the most (Tideiksaar, 1998). With diminished strength, a greater number of muscle fibers must be activated to perform a task (Pescatello & Judge, 1995). Hence, what may have taken only 6% of muscle reserves to accomplish a task, such as arising from a chair, may now require 60% (Pescatello & Judge, 1995). As the reserve of strength required to perform a task becomes greater, so does the perceived difficulty in carrying out the task. Consequently, the very old may be less likely to engage in this task (Pescatello & Judge, 1995).

Muscle strengthening and aerobic exercise, particularly involving the lower extremities, increase muscle strength. Simple strength training exercises can be done in the home without equipment when the weight of the body or limb is used as resistance (Topp, Mikesky, Wigglesworth, Holt, & Edwards, 1993). Under supervision, even high-intensity strength training has been found to improve strength and, subsequently, walking speed and getting out of a chair among frail institutionalized elders in their 80s and 90s (Fiatarone et al., 1990; Schilke, Johnson, Housh, & O'Dell, 1996). Moreover, strength training of the lower extremities resulted in greater function and lower pain that may contribute to independence in ADL (Maurer, Stern, Kinossian, Cook, & Schumacher, 1999). Aerobic exercise can also improve strength of the muscles involved in the activity (Ades, Maloney, Savage, & Carhart, 1999). Walking is an aerobic activity that most oldest-old can participate in safely and easily (Roberts, 1989).

Balance

Balance involves the control of the body during movement, and limitations in balance have been associated with falls (Clark, Lord, & Webster, 1993; Pescatello & Judge, 1995), abnormalities in gait (Rantanen, Guralnik, Ferrucci, et al., 1999), disability (Rantanen, Guralnik, Sakari-Rantala, et al., 1999), and dependence in ADL (Roberts & Wykle, 1993). Various types of exercise can improve balance, and these include aerobic exercise (Roberts, 1989; Roberts, Srour, Mansour, Palmer, & Wagner, 1984), muscle strengthening (Moxley Scarborough, Krebs, & Harris, 1998), and tai chi (Tse & Bailey, 1992). Balance training that involves stressing the balance system in a controlled environment has also been found to improve balance (Hu & Woollacott, 1994a, b).

Gait

Gait is essential in safe movement as well as for mobility and transferring from sitting, lying, and standing positions (Hu & Woollacott, 1995). Abnormal patterns and characteristics of gait have been associated with falls (Chen, Ashton-Miller, Alexander, & Schultz, 1991; Clark et al., 1993; Tideiksaar, 1998) and recovery of mobility (Friedman, Rickmond, & Basket, 1988). Exercise such as aerobic walking (Roberts, Srour, et al., 1994), muscle strengthening (Topp et al., 1993; Moxley Scarborough et al., 1998), and tai chi (Tse & Bailey, 1992) has been found to positively affect gait. In these examples, the exercises used can easily be taught and done safely by the oldest-old in their own homes.

Cognitive Impairment

Cognitive impairment significantly predicts dependence in daily activities (Hill, Backman, & Fratiglioni, 1995). Cognitive impairment can be reflected in many arenas that include memory, following instructions, recognizing figures and words, attention, and orientation to time, place, and person. Interventions that provide the oldest-old with an opportunity to use cognitive skills have been effective and were developed from information psychology (Grasel, 1994), information and processing theory (Rosswurm, 1989), environmental meaning and legibility (Algase et al., 1996; Roberts & Algase, 1988), and progressively lowered stress threshold (Hall et al., 1995). These interventions include memory exercises (Bourgeois, 1992; Camp et al., 1993) and memory aids (Bourgeois, 1992), tasks with familiar stimuli (Quayhagen & Quayhagen, 1989), priming (McKitrick, Camp, & Black, 1995), and constructing an environment consistent with the cognitive abilities of the very old (Hall et al., 1995). The very old can do some of these interventions by themselves; others require help from a caregiver or health-care provider.

Depression and Well-Being

Often depression is unrecognized in elderly adults because the symptoms are different in elders than they are in younger adults (Buckwalter, 1992; Heston et al., 1992) or due to ageism and stereotypes (Beck, Cronin-Stubbs, Buckwalter, & Rapp, 1999). Because depression can often be overlooked, assessment is essential among the oldest-old, who may be reluctant to discuss their feelings of depression with their health-care provider or family. Using cognitive theory, efforts to change the self-talk of the oldest-old from self-deprecatory to self-affirming can be effective. Behavioral approaches include positive reinforcement of self-affirming behavior; interpersonal approaches focus on improving the social relationships with significant others in the social network of the very old. The long-term effects of these interventions are not known (Agency for Health Care Policy and Research, 1993), and no one intervention is superior to another (Schneider, 1995; Scogin & McElreath, 1994).

Results of our study add another dimension to understanding depression among the old: that of having a future time orientation. When these very old people had goals consistently, their sense of well-being was greater. They were more depressed when they had goals at one time but then did not have goals at another time point.

One possible explanation is that of control that having goals may help elders feel more in control of their lives and thus contribute to better mental health. Fostering a goal orientation could therefore be very helpful.

We also considered self-perception among our respondents. We found that when they compared themselves with others who were not doing as well, it had a positive influence on how they saw themselves. Helping those who are very old see the silver lining could be of value in boosting self-imagine. Interestingly, we also found that just being over 90 had its own reward. That factor alone often made the respondent feel special and fortunate, emotions that are beneficial to a sense of well-being.

Functional Limitations

Functional limitations of the lower extremities are more strongly associated with dependence in IADLs; dependence in ADLs is more strongly associated with limitations in the upper extremities (Lawrence & Jette, 1996; Jette et al., 1990). Because functional limitations can arise from sources other than pathology, factors amenable to change should be the focus of interventions.

High body mass and frequency of walking a mile were predictors of functional limitations (Lawrence & Jette, 1996), whereas greater muscle strength was related to greater stride length and gait velocity and more efficient arising from a chair (Moxley Scarborough et al., 1998). Hence, a weight loss intervention and exercise may reduce functional limitations. Moreover, muscle strengthening exercise reduced reliance on assistive devices for walking and improved the ability and frequency of arising from a chair (Fiatarone et al., 1990; Schilke et al., 1996) and distance walked (Topp et al., 1993). Exercise also increased mobility (Koroknay, Werner, Cohen-Mansfield, & Braun, 1995).

Motor retraining can improve performance of a functional task. For example, repeated practice recovering from trips or unstable surfaces increases the ability to regain postural control and prevents a fall during usual activities (Hu & Woollacott, 1994a, b). Chair exercises also increased the abilities of older adults to arise from a chair and sit down (McMurdo & Rennie, 1993).

Modification of the environment affects how a task is performed and can improve functional abilities. Replacing low overstuffed chairs with harder and higher chairs or a motorized chair may allow the very old to arise from a chair as well as sit down. Grasping devices and footstools can be used to reach objects that the oldest-old are unable to reach on their own. Grab bars enable the very old to move from lying, sitting, and standing positions and stabilize them when performing such tasks such as climbing stairs or reaching. Structural alterations such as lowered cupboards, increased light intensity, and doorways widened to accommodate a wheel chair can be used to tailor the physical environment to accommodate any incapabilities of older adults and contribute to their independence (Hall et al., 1995; Lawton & Nahemow, 1973; Lawton, 1982).

However, the very old may have the functional capabilities to perform the ADL but still require assistance. The role of decisions that elderly adults make about whether and how they will engage in daily behaviors has been ignored but has important implications for assessment and interventions (Roberts, 1999). The congruence between physical capabilities and actual performance has been moderate at best (Cress et al., 1995; Mendes de Leon, Seeman, Baker, Richardson, & Tinetti, 1996; Roberts, 1989). The fear of falling and lowered self-efficacy also has been associated with increased disability (Mendes de Leon et al., 1996; Seeman, Unger, McAvay, & Mendes de Leon, 1999; Tinetti, Mendes de Leon, Doucette, & Baker, 1994). Those who are cognitively impaired may overestimate their abilities, whereas depressed adults underestimate their abilities (Roberts et al., 1993; Roberts, 1999). Interventions to reduce depression and cognitive impairment and to assist the very old to evaluate their physical capabilities accurately have the potential to increase the independence of these individuals (Roberts, 1999).

An understanding of the multiple factors associated with the performance of daily activities is required to target interventions and services. Disease alone is not a sensitive indicator of functional limitation or disability, and a certain amount of improvement in impairments and functional limitations must take place before disability can be reduced (Roberts, 1999).

Knowing the underlying risk factors for dependence can help identify those at highest risk so that interventions and services appropriate for a specific risk factor can be applied. Interventions and services can then be targeted to those elders who would benefit most, which is very important when interventions are costly and time consuming for the health-care provider and elderly adult. Significant changes in underlying factors associated with independence may be needed before any change is possible in complex tasks of daily living. Hence, the effects of interventions on underlying impairments and functional limitations may be significant. Yet, the effects on disability may be smaller and may emerge only when effects are large enough to overcome thresholds in impairments and functional limitations (Roberts, 1999). A multiplicity of environmental, physical, and psychological factors contribute to independence, and interventions and services must address most, if not all, of them.

SUMMARY AND CONCLUSION

In our study, we examined the everyday lives of the oldest-old, what they believed about themselves, stresses, personal resources to deal with stressors, and their functional health. We found that even at 85 years of age and older, many of our respondents were active and able to live independently and continued to have goals and aspirations. There was only a moderate change in independence in ADL and IADL, mainly due to the fact that we started with a community-dwelling sample. Interestingly, as dependence in these activities increased so did the worries of daily life, suggesting that these limitations may make dealing with the common occurrences of daily life more difficult because of dwindling physical resources. Although support from others in the social network may mitigate worry, the social network of these very old respondents declined over time. Given the advanced age of our respondents, their children, who often provide the primary support to the parents, were older adults themselves whose poor health and disability could preclude them from providing assistance as needed. Indeed, the oldest-old in our study relied heavily on friends and neighbors who might be less likely to assume a significant amount of care and assistance that family members are more likely to provide. Overall, our elders did not report a significant decline in support.

Although the social network of our respondents declined, there was no significant decline in support. This seems unusual and may be due to the measures of support that were used in this study. We were able to determine if someone was available to provide various services and the frequency of contact. Even with the death of family members, support was provided by neighbors and friends. What we do not know is how our elders felt about the declining network of family members and what impact this had on the quality of their lives. Qualitative research would be very helpful here.

Among our very old respondents, mortality was related to being male, depressed, and worried and having poorer perceived health. Because depression increased over time, whereas perceived health changed little, interventions to reduce depression, even with advancing age but stable health, may reduce mortality in these individuals. Depression and dependence in ADL may make daily life more difficult; improving these could make life more enjoyable for the very old and reduce the worry of everyday life.

Through our study we learned about the lives and physical and mental conditions of the very old. More research is required to understand how perceptual, social, and personal resources and psychological well-being, as well as physical condition, contribute to a productive and enjoyable life among the very old, and in particular the very old as they grow older. Longitudinal work with a larger sample is needed to better understand the issues that these elders and their subsequent service providers face in fostering a greater sense of well-being and productivity.

In conclusion, the very old are increasing in numbers and the boundaries of the life span are increasing as well. There is no doubt that the needs of the very old will tax existing financial and support systems. This trend is apparent even with an initial sample that included elders who were living in the community. More research is needed to understand the life circumstances of the very old and how to increase their quality of life and independence in daily activities into their 80s and 90s. As noted earlier, numerous potential interventions, which are not disease specific, can contribute to lower disability and greater independence in daily activities. Without further attention to these issues, the governmental and social resources of this country will be greatly taxed or, in all likelihood, unable to meet the needs of this growing segment of the population of the United States.

Appendix

METHODS

This book presents data from a longitudinal study of persons 85 years and older from five interviews over a 9-year period. Respondents were interviewed four times every 6 months and again 9 years after the initial interview in 1986. The interviews focused on their life circumstances, health, disability, stressors and worries, and coping strategies and resources. The sample at Wave 1 in the present study represents urban elderly adults living independently in the Cleveland, Ohio, area. As such, generalizations to the very old living in rural areas, assisted living facilities, and long-term care facilities cannot be made.

SETTING AND SAMPLE SELECTION

In the Cleveland metropolitan area, 193 subjects were recruited in 1986 from a variety of noninstitutional sources. Because residence in nursing homes rapidly rises with age (U.S. Department of Health and Human Services, 1989), this community sample underrepresents the total population of the oldest-old; hence, generalizations can only be made to the oldest-old who live in the community. The waiting lists of two multilevel care facilities where the oldest-old lived independently (17.1%) were used for recruitment, as well as nutrition sites and Golden Age Senior Centers (30.1%). This mixture of sites was chosen to ensure adequate diversity on key control variables such as socioeconomic status and race. Subjects attending nutrition programs may have greater social support, and they were included in the sampling plan to ensure variability. To recruit the very old who do not attend these activities, persons 85 and older were identified from publicly available Homestead Exemption Lists for property taxes in nine cities (23.3%). Twelve percent were recruited from a registry of elderly persons interested in participating in research studies, and 15.5% were from referrals by other subjects.

The 147 women and 46 men, ranging in age from 84 to 99 years, had a mean age of 87.7 years (SD = 2.72). Sixty percent ($n = 117$) of the sample had a high school education or less, and 17.6 percent ($n = 34$) were black. Twenty-one percent of subjects ($n = 40$) were married, 70.5% ($n = 136$) were widowed, and 8.8% ($n = 17$), who were divorced or single, were all women.

The sample for this study was compared to a random sample obtained from the Medicare lists for the Cleveland area in 1975 (Ford, Haug, Roy, & Folmar, 1992). This study comprised 1598 persons 65 years of age and older. In 1984, 471 subjects had survived, and 162 were 85 years of age or older. The sample in the present study was representative of this age group because it was similar to a 1975 representative sample, and changes during this subsequent 11-year period would be representative (Ford et al., 1992). Cleveland is a typical city that had little migration during this period (Gurwitz & Kingsley, 1982), and the biasing effects of migration were minimal.

The demographic characteristics were similar to the Cleveland random sample (Ford et al., 1992). In the Cleveland sample, the average age was 88.5 years, similar to the average of 87.7 years in this study. Compared with the Cleveland sample, there were greater proportions of men and blacks (30% and 29%, respectively) than in the current study (23.8% and 17.6%, respectively). Although this study had demographic characteristics similar to the random sample, there were some differences, and the findings should be interpreted with this in mind.

Each respondent was asked to participate in four home interviews spaced 6 months apart. These intervals maximized information gained while minimizing attrition. The 18-month time period was sufficiently long to ensure time for change in independence in this old-old age group. A follow-up interview was done 7 years after the last of these interviews.

The data from five interviews are presented in this book. The initial baseline interview is Wave 1 ($n = 193$). During the 18 months after baseline, subjects were interviewed three more times: Wave 2 ($n = 180$), Wave 3 ($n = 163$), and Wave 4 ($n = 155$). At Wave 5 ($n = 23$), subjects were interviewed again, which was 9 years after the initial interview.

Attrition and Survival

Because attrition related to deaths was expected in this very old sample, information about death was obtained from significant others and validated by death certificate. If unable to confirm whether the subject had died, the death certificates from Ohio from the last day of testing to the time of data analysis were reviewed. Between Wave 1 and Wave 4, there were 44 confirmed deaths, and between Wave 4 and Wave 5, there were 102.

During the initial 18-month study period, 23 respondents died and 16 were either too ill or no longer interested in participating or had moved outside the 50-mile radius of our study site. Nine years after the baseline interview, 102 subjects had died and 68 subjects were unable to be interviewed because of their physical or cognitive status. Twenty-three subjects survived to the Wave 5 interview, and 131 survived to the Wave 4 but not Wave 5 interview (155 interviewed at Wave 4 minus the 23 interviewed at Wave 5). Table A.1 shows a

TABLE A.1 Number of Subjects Interviewed and Attrition

Status	Wave 1 ($n = 193$) 1985–1986	Wave 2 ($n = 180$) 1986	Wave 3 ($n = 163$) 1986–1987	Wave 4 ($n = 154$) 1987	Wave 5 ($n = 23$) 1994–1995
Interviewed	193	180	163	155	23
Died	NA	6	8	7	102
Refused or unable to be interviewed	NA	7	22	31	68

NA, not applicable

summary of reasons for attrition and the total number of respondents interviewed at each wave of data collection.

VARIABLES AND MEASURES

The lives of the very old and consequences of stress were the foci of this study. Although little is known about the oldest-old, the age of subjects involved in this research precluded the development of an extensive interview schedule. Therefore, the selected variables were the key concepts necessary for the analysis. Not all variables were measured at Wave 5 because the extreme age and frailty of the respondents limited the duration of the interview.

STRESS

Stressors related to life events were measured by the Geriatric Scale of Recent Life Events (Kahana et al., 1982). This scale consists of 23 items from the Social Readjustment Scale (Holmes & Rahe, 1967) and 32 items relevant to the life experiences of elderly persons. The respondents indicated only events that occurred in the last year. Because life events can be positive or negative, the items were categorized as such. There were 25 negative events related to illness, functional and physical impairment, death of significant others, change in residence, relationships, and belongings. Four positive events were included (birth of a child, marriage in the family, personal achievement of a family member, and improvement in a family member's health). The events that occurred in the last year were summed for negative stressors (range of 0 to 25) and for positive stressors (range of 0 to 4). Measures of internal consistency are not appropriate here because these events are discrete.

Worries related to everyday events were measured by the Hassles Scale (Kanner et al., 1981). Because persons in the sample used in the Kanner study were not over the age 64, the items were screened for relevance to those age 85 and over, and 23 items relevant to the very old were used. Subjects rated the severity of each hassle occurring during the previous month from 0, "not at all"; 1, "a little"; and 2, "a great deal." The ratings were summed for a score. Kanner et al. (1981) found that hassles were strongly associated with adaptational outcomes. Although daily hassles overlap considerably with life events, they also operate quite strongly and independently of life events in predicting psychological symptoms. Although there have been some suggestions that these items are confounded with psychopathology, evidence to the contrary has been found (Lazarus et al., 1985; see Roberts et al., 1994 for a discussion of these issues). At the initial interview, Cronbach's alpha was 0.84.

PSYCHOLOGICAL COPING RESOURCES

Self-esteem is a reflection of the individual's evaluation of self-worth and can be a resource in coping with the challenges of life (Rodin, 1989). Self-esteem was measured by Rosenberg Self-Esteem Scale consisting of 10 items scored as a Guttman scale (Rosenberg, 1965). The subjects rated each item as applicable to them or not, and the ratings were summed for a score. The index has discriminate validity (Silber & Tippett, 1965) and a reproducibility coefficient of 0.92 (Rosenberg, 1965). At Wave 1, Cronbach's alpha was 0.91.

Mastery over events represents the perceived control an individual has over events and circumstances in their lives (Pearlin & Schooler, 1978). Mastery was measured by the seven-item Pearlin Mastery Scale (Pearlin & Schooler, 1978). Respondents rated their control over events from 0, "not at all" to 3, "strongly agree." This scale had very low reliability (Cronbach's alpha = 0.35) in this study. To ascertain whether this was due to inconsistency of responses among the very old or multiple dimensions in this measure, principal components factor analysis was performed (Roberts, Dunkle, et al., 1994). Three factors were extracted. The first factor, Global Perceived Control, accounted for 27.1% of the variance and included four items: "no way to solve a problem," "control of things that happen," "feelings of helplessness," and "ability to change things in life." The second factor, Perceived Ability to Control Events, accounted for 17.3% of the variance and contained only one item, "perceived control over events." The third factor, Locus of Control, accounted for 16.5% of the variance and contained two items: "ability to control the future" and "feelings of being pushed around." Cronbach's alpha for the first factor was 0.62. The Cronbach's alpha for the third factor was low, 0.16, and this factor was not used in the analyses. Cronbach's alpha for the second factor is not appropriate because it consisted of one item.

SOCIAL COPING RESOURCES

Social support embodies social resources and involves the interaction between people. It has most frequently been conceptualized as the provision of tangible support, although emotional support has also been identified.

Availability of social support for companionship and assistance from others, which represented the size of the social network but not the support actually received, was measured using items from the OARS instrument (Duke University Center for the Study of Aging and Human Development, 1978). Respondents indicated whether there was someone they could confide in and a person who could provide occasional, short-term or long-term assistance. Categories were summed for a score ranging from 0 to 5. Cronbach's alpha was 0.54 in the present study at Wave 1.

Frequency of social interactions with others was measured using items from the OARS (Duke University, 1978). Respondents noted the number of friends whom they knew well to visit (0, "none"; 1, "one to 2"; 2, "3 to 4"; 3, "5 or more") and the number of times a week of social contact by phone and visits (0, "none"; 1, "once a week"; 2, "2 to 6 times a week"; 3, "once a day or more"). These ratings were summed for a score ranging from 0 to 12. At Wave 1, Cronbach's alpha was 0.54.

COPING STRATEGIES

Coping strategies were assessed by an episodic, process-focused view of coping, explored using open-ended questions. The respondents were asked what they did when they felt worried or concerned about something and how they solved problems. The first two strategies mentioned were coded into one of eight categories identified by Folkman et al. (1986). Problem-focused coping strategies focus on managing or solving a stressful situation. Confronting the problem involves aggressive efforts that support risk taking or hostility. Seeking social support involves emotional and informational comfort from others. When individuals accept responsibility, they acknowledge the role that they played in the stressful situation. Planful problem-solving involves deliberate efforts to alter the situation.

In contrast, emotion-focused coping strategies are employed to manage the emotional reactions to stress. In distancing, the individual detaches from the situation or develops a positive outlook about the situation. Escape-avoidance involves efforts to avoid the stressful situation or event or wishful thinking. Personal growth is the focus of positive reappraisal that may have a religious tone. Table A.2 provides a summary of the coding scheme for each strategy.

A weighted index of coping was constructed, with the first mention of a strategy scored 2 and the second mention of it scored as 1. Instrumental or problem-solving coping was confrontive, seeking social support, accepting responsibility, and problem-solving strategies. Emotion-focused coping included distancing, self-control, escape-avoidance, and positive reappraisal. Responses to the questions were scored 0 for emotion-focused strategies and 1 for problem-focused strategies. The scored ranged from 0 to 6, with higher scores indicating problem-focused coping. Interrater reliability was 0.93 at the first interview.

HEALTH AND DISABILITY

Physical health was obtained by self-report. On a 4-point scale ranging from 0, "poor," to 3, "excellent," respondents rated their present health. Using a rating scale of 1, "worse"; 2, "about the same;" or 3, "better," respondents rated their present health as compared with 5 years earlier and as compared with others their own age. A health index was computed by summing the ratings of health. Whereas many elaborate measures of physical health are available, these self-rated scores were significantly related to other measures of health (Rosencranz & Philblad, 1970). The criterion-related validity of these ratings is supported because they strongly predict survival (Idler & Angel, 1990). In addition, information about chronic conditions was obtained.

TABLE A.2   Content Coding for Coping Strategies

Problem-focused coping to manage or solve a stressful situation

Confrontive: Aggressive efforts that support risk tak- ing or hostility	By getting mad. Then I rationalize. I am independent and told that I am stubborn. I figure what is mine is mine. My word should be the one used.
Seeking social support: Seek informational and emotional com- fort from others	Sought advice from someone Talked with someone about the problem Depends on the seriousness of the prob- lem. . . . I'd go to my daughter or my practitioner.
Accepting responsibility: Acknowledge the role that he or she played in the stressful situation	I always take advice, but following it is another thing.
Planful problem-solving: Deliberate efforts to alter the situation	Made a plan to solve the problem Well, you just use your common sense. If something comes up—you can sort of analyze it, if that's possible. Well, sometimes I solve them.

Emotion-focused coping strategies to manage the emotional reactions to stress

Distancing: Detach from the situation or develop a positive outlook	I put things in the back of my mind. I am able to adjust, as I said before. I don't let anything bother me.
Escape-avoidance: Efforts to avoid the stressful situation or event or wishful thinking	Sometimes I'll take a little hi-ball if I can't solve it. I do a lot of thinking and daydreaming.
Positive reappraisal: Personal growth and may have reli- gious undertones	I prayed, and it works. If something is going one way, it will. I don't just drop it, but I confess prayer has a lot to do with it. Looked on the bright side

Mental health was assessed by self-ratings, the Bradburn Affect Balance Scale, a global measure of mental health (Bradburn, 1969), and the Derogotis Depression Scale (Derogatis, 1977).

The Bradburn Affect Balance Scale is based on the model of two independent factors to mental health: negative and positive. Bradburn (1969) suggested that the best indicator of mental health was the balance between these two factors. Hence, the score is the difference of the summed ratings for the positive and negative sub-scales, with 5 added to obtain a range from 0 to 10. Cronbach's alpha in this study was 0.97 at the initial interview.

On a four-point scale ranging from 0, "poor," to 3, "excellent," respondents rated their present mental health. Using a rating scale of 1, "worse"; 2, "about the same"; or 3, "better," respondents rated their present mental health compared with 5 years earlier (Waves 1 and 5) or 6 months earlier (Waves 2 to 4) and as compared with others their own age. A mental health index was computed by summing the ratings.

Depression was measured by the Derogotis SCL-90 Depression Scale (Derogatis, 1977). Respondents ranked items as 0, "not at all"; 1, "a little"; 2, "moderate"; 3, "quite a bit"; and 4, "extremely." Items included hopelessness about the future, thoughts of ending life and of worthlessness, and feelings of tenseness, fearfulness, and nervousness. The rankings were summed. Scores ranged from 0 to 24, with higher scores indicating greater depression. At Wave 1, Cronbach's alpha was 0.87.

FUNCTIONAL ABILITIES: ACTIVITIES OF DAILY LIVING

Basic ADLs were measured by the Katz Index of Activities of Daily Living (Katz et al., 1963), which assesses assistance required in bathing, feeding, dressing, transfer, toileting, and continence. The respondents ranked each task from 0, "unable," to 2 ,"able." The ratings were summed for a score ranging from 0 to 12, with higher scores indicating greater independence. Katz and Akpom (1976) established the validity of this index and found reproducibility coefficients of 0.95 to 0.98, and Cronbach's alpha during the first interview was 0.67.

IADLs were measured by items from the OARS survey (Duke University, 1978). The activities assessed were those needed to live independently and included handling finances, using the phone, taking medication, mobility, shopping, preparing meals, and doing housework (Fillenbaum, 1988). Respondents rated each item as 0, "unable"; 1, "with some help"; and 2, "unable." Rankings were summed for a score ranging from 0 to 14, with higher scores indicating greater impairment. The reliability and validity of this scale has been well-established. At Wave 1, Cronbach's alpha was 0.91.

References

Abeles, R., Gift, H., & Ory, M. (Eds.). (1994). *Aging and quality of life.* New York: Springer.

Ades, P. A., Ballor, D. L., Ashikaga, T., Utton, J. L., & Nair, K. S. (1996). Weight training improves walking endurance in healthy elderly persons. *Annals of Internal Medicine, 124,* 568–572.

Ades, P. A., Maloney, A., Savage, P., & Carhart, R. L. (1999). Determinants of physical functioning in coronary patients: Response to cardiac rehabilitation. *Archives of Internal Medicine, 159,* 2357–2360.

Agency for Health Care Policy and Research. (1993). *Depression in primary care (Vol. 2: Treatment of major depression)* (AHCPR Publication No. 93-0551). Washington, DC: U.S. Government Printing Office.

Aiken, L. S., & West, S. G. (1991). *Multiple regression: Testing and interpreting interactions.* London: Sage.

Albert, S. (1977). Temporal comparison theory. *Psychological Review, 84,* 485–503.

Aldwin, C. M., Levenson, M. R., Spiro, A. F., & Bosse, R. (1989). Does emotionality predict stress? Findings from the Normative Aging Study. *Journal of Personality and Social Psychology, 56,* 618–624.

Aldwin, C. M., & Revenson, T. (1986). Vulnerability to economic stress. *American Journal of Community Psychology, 14,* 161–175.

Aldwin, C. M., Sutton, K. J., & Lachman, M. (1996). The development of coping resources in adulthood. *Journal of Personality, 64,* 837–871.

Algase, D. L., Beck, C., Kolanowski, A., Whall, A., Berent, S., Richards, K., & Beattie, E. (1996). Need-driven dementia-compromised behavior: An alternative view of disruptive behavior. *American Journal of Alzheimer's Care and Related Disorders and Research, 11,* 12–19.

151

Aneshensel, C., Frerichs, R., Clark, V., & Yokopenic, P. (1982). Telephone versus in person surveys of community health status. *American Journal of Public Health, 72,* 1017–1021.

Antonucci, T. C. (1986). Measuring social support networks: Hierarchical mapping technique. *Generations, 10.*

Antonucci, T. C., Fuhrer, R., & Dartigues, J. (1997). Social relations and depressive symptomatology in a sample of community-dwelling French older adults. *Psychology and Aging, 12,* 189–195.

Arean, P. A., Robinson, G., & Hicks, S. (1997, November). *Mental illness in minority elderly: Prevalence and use of services.* Presented at the 50th annual scientific meeting of the Geriatric Society of America.

Arfkin, C. L., Lash, H. W., Birge, S. J., & Miller, J. P. (1994). The prevalence and correlates of fear of falling in elderly persons living in the community. *American Journal of Public Health, 84,* 565–570.

Atchley, R. C. (1982). The aging self. *Psychotherapy: Theory, Research, and Practice, 19,* 338–396.

Baltes, M. M., & Carstensen, L. L. (1996). The process of successful aging. *Ageing and Society, 16,* 397–422.

Bandura, A. (1981). Self-referent thought: A developmental analysis of self-efficacy. In J. H. Riley & L. Ross (Eds.), *Social cognitive development: Frontiers and possible futures* (pp. 200–239). New York: Cambridge University Press.

Bassey, E. J. (1998). Longitudinal changes in selected physical capabilities: Muscle strength, flexibility and body size. *Age and Ageing, 27*(suppl), 12–16.

Beck, C., Cronin-Stubbs, D., Buckwalter, K. C., & Rapp, C. G. (1999). Cognitive impairment and depression in the elderly. In A. S. Hinshaw, S. L. Feetham, & J. L. F. Shaver (Eds.), *Handbook of clinical nursing research* (pp. 579–597). London: Sage.

Bienenfeld, D., Koenig, H. G., Larson, D. B., & Sherrill, K. A. (1997). Psychosocial predictors of mental health in a population of elderly women. Test of an explanatory model. *American Journal of Geriatric Psychiatry, 5,* 43–53.

Blaney, P. H. (1985). Stress and coping. In T. M. Field, P. M. McCabe, & N. Schniederman (Eds.), *Stress and depression in adults: A critical review* (pp. 263–283). Hillsdale, NJ: Erlbaum.

Blazer, D. (1983). The epidemiology of depression in late life. In L. Breslau & M. Haug (Eds.), *Depression and aging* (pp. 30–50). New York: Springer.

Blazer, D. (1993). *Depression in late life* (2nd ed.). St. Louis: Mosby-Year Book.

Blazer, D. G. (1982). Social support and mortality in an elderly population. *American Journal of Epidemiology, 115,* 684–694.

Blazer, D. G., Hughes, D. C., & George, L. K. (1987). The epidemiology of depression in an elderly community population. *Gerontologist, 27,* 281–287.

Bonderik, M., & Stogstad, A. (1998). The oldest old, ADL, social network and loneliness. *Western Journal of Nursing Research, 20,* 325–343.

Bondevik, M., & Skogstad, A. (1995). The oldest old and personal activities of daily living. *Scandinavian Journal of Caring Sciences, 9,* 219–226.

Bould, S., Sanborn, B., & Reif, L. (1988). *Eighty-five plus: The oldest old.* Belmont, CA: Wadsworth.

Boult, C., Boult, L., Murphy, C., Ebbitt, B., Luptak, M., & Kane, R. (1994). A controlled trial of outpatient geriatric evaluation and management. *Journal of the American Geriatrics Society, 42,* 465–470.

Bourgeois, M. S. (1992). Evaluating memory wallets in conversations with persons with dementia. *Journal of Speech and Hearing Research, 35,* 1344–1357.

Bradburn, N. M. (1969). *The structure of psychological well-being.* Chicago: Aldine.

Brandtstadter, J. (1992). Personal control over development: Some developmental implications of self-efficacy. In R. Schwarzer (Ed.), *Self efficacy: Thought control of action* (pp. 127–145). Washington, DC: Hemisphere.

Brandtstadter, J., & Baltes-Gotz, B. (1990). Personal control over development and quality of life perspectives in adulthood. In P. B. Baltes & M. M. Baltes (Eds.), *Successful aging: Perspectives from behavioral sciences* (pp. 197–224). Cambridge: Cambridge University Press.

Brandtstadter, J., & Greve, W. (1994). The aging self: Stabilizing and protective processes. *Developmental Review, 14,* 52–80.

Brandtstadter, J., & Rothermund, K. (1994). Self-perception of control in middle and later adulthood: Buffering losses by rescaling goals. *Psychology and Aging, 9,* 265–273.

Brandtstadter, J., Wentura, D., & Greve, W. (1993). Adaptive resources of the aging self: Outlines of an emergent perspective. *International Journal of Behavioral Development, 16,* 323–349.

Breytspraak, L. M. (1984). *The development of self in later life.* Toronto: Little, Brown & Company.

Brim, G. (1992). *Ambition: How we manage success and failure throughout our lives.* New York: Basic Books.

Buckwalter, K. C. (1992). *Geriatric mental health nursing: Current and future challenges.* Thorofare, NJ: Slack.

Bureau of the Census. (1994). *Statistical Abstract of the United States* (114 ed.). Washington, DC: U.S. Government Printing Office.

Bureau of the Census. (1995). *Statistical Abstract of the United States* (115 ed.). Washington, DC: U.S. Government Printing Office.

Bureau of the Census. (1997). *Statistical Abstract of the United States* (117 ed.). Washington, DC: U.S. Government Printing Office.

Burke, M., & Flaherty, M. J. (1993). Coping strategies and health status of elderly arthritic women. *Journal of Advanced Nursing, 18,* 7–13.

Burton, R. G. (1976). The human awareness of time: An analysis. *Philosophy and Phenomenological Research* XXXVI, 303–318.

Bury, M., & Holme, A. (1991). *Life after ninety.* London: Routledge.

Caldwell, R., & Reinhart, M. (1988). The relationships of personality to individual differences in the use of type and source of social support. *Journal of Social and Clinical Psychology, 6,* 140–146.

Callahan, C. M., Hendrie, H. C., Dittus, R. S., Brater, D. C., Hui, S. L., & Tierney, W. M. (1994). Improving treatment in late life depression in primary care: A randomized clinical trial. *Journal of the American Geriatrics Society, 42,* 839–845.

Camacho, T., Strawbridge, W., Cohen, R., & Kaplan, G. (1993). Functional ability in the oldest old. *Journal of Aging and Health, 5,* 439–454.

Camp, C. J., Foss, J. W., Stevens, A. B., Reichard, C. C., McKitrick, L. A., & O'Hanlon, A. M. (1993). Memory training in normal and demented elderly populations: The E-I-E-I-O model. *Experimental Aging Research, 19,* 277–290.

Cantor, N., & Kihlstrom, J. F. (1987). *Personality and social intelligence.* Engelwood Cliffs, NJ: Prentice Hall.

Carlson, M., Berg, S., & Wenestan, C. G. (1991). The oldest old: Patterns of adjustment and dependence. *Scandinavian Journal of Caring Science, 5,* 93–100.

Carnes, B., & Olshansky, S. (1993). Evolutionary perspectives on human senescence. *Population and Development Review, 19,* 793–806.

Carstensen, L., & Freund, A. (1994). The resilience of the aging self. *Developmental Review, 14,* 81–92.

Carver, C., & Scheier, M. (1990). Origins and functions of positive and negative affect: A control-process view. *Psychological Review, 97,* 19–25.

Case, R. (1991). Development of self: Stages in the development of the young child's first sense of self. *Developmental Review, 11,* 210–230.

Chen, H. C., Ashton-Miller, J. A., Alexander, N. B., & Schultz, A. B. (1991). Stepping over obstacles: Gait patterns of healthy young and old adults. *Journals of Gerontology: Medical Sciences, 46,* M196–M203.

Chipperfield, J. (1993). Incongruence between health perceptions and health problems. *Journal of Aging and Health, 5,* 475–496.

Chiriboga, D. A. (1992). Paradise lost: Stress in the modern age. In M. L. Wykle, E. Kahana, & J. Kowal (Eds.), *Stress and health among the elderly* (pp. 35–71). New York: Springer.

Cho, C. Y., Alessi, C. A., Cho, M., Aronow, H. U., Stuck, A. E., Rubenstein, L. Z., & Beck, J. C. (1998). The association between chronic illness and functional change among participants in a comprehensive geriatric assessment program. *Journal of the American Geriatric Society, 46,* 677–682.

Clark, R. D., Lord, S. R., & Webster, I. W. (1993). Clinical parameters associated with falls in an elderly population. *Gerontology, 39,* 117–123.

Clark, D., Maddox, G., & Steinhauser, K. (1993). Racing, aging and functional health. *Journal of Aging and Health, 5,* 536–553.

Cohen, L. H., Towbes, L. C., & Flocco, R. (1988). Effects of induced mood on self-reported life events and perceived and received social support. *Journal of Personality and Social Psychology, 55,* 669–674.

Cohen, M. A., Tell, E. J., & Wallack, S. S. (1986). Client-related risk factors of nursing home entry among elderly adults. *Journal of Gerontology, 41,* 785–792.

Cohen, S., Tyrrell, D. A., & Smith, A. P. (1993). Negative life events, perceived stress, negative affect, and susceptibility to the common cold. *Journal of Personality and Social Psychology, 64,* 131–140.

Cole, M. G., & Bellavance, F. (1997). The prognosis of depression in old age. *American Journal of Geriatric Psychiatry, 5,* 4–14.

Cooley, C. H. (1902). *Human nature and the social order.* New York: Charles Scribners.

Cooper, J., & Goethals, G. R. (1981). The self concept of old age. In J. N. Morgan, S. B. Kiesler, & V. K. Oppenheimer (Eds.), *Aging social change* (pp. 431–452). New York: Academic Press.

Corey-Bloom, J., Wilderholt, W., Edelstein, S., & Salmon, D. (1996). Cognitive and functional status of the oldest old. *Journal of the American Geriatrics Society, 44,* 671–674.

Coroni-Huntley, J. C., Foley, D. J., White, L. R., Suzman, R. M., Berkman, L. F., Evans, D. A., Wallace, R. B., & Branch, L. G. (1992). Epidemiology of disability in the oldest old. In R. M. Suzman, D. P. Willis, & K. Manton (Eds.), *The oldest old* (pp. 268–282). New York: Oxford Press.

Costa, P., & Kastenbaum, R. (1967). Some aspects of memories and ambitions in centenarians. *Journal of Genetic Psychology, 110,* 3–16.

Costa, P., & McCrae, R. (1993). Handbook of stress: Theoretical and clinical aspects. In L. Goldberger & S. Breznitz (Eds.), *Psychological stress and coping in old age* (pp. 403–412). New York: The Free Press.

Coyne, J. C., Aldwin, C., & Lazarus, R. S. (1999). Depression and coping in stressful episodes. *Journal of Abnormal Psychology, 90,* 439–447.

Craft, B., Johnson, D., & Ortega, S. (1998). Rural-urban women's experience of symptoms of depression related to economic hardship. *Journal of Women and Aging, 10*(3), 3–18.

Cress, M. E., Schechtman, K. B., Mulrow, R. D., Fiatarone, M. A., Gerety, M. B., & Buchner, D. M. (1995). Relationship between physical performance and self-perceived physical function. *Journal of the American Geriatrics Society, 43,* 93–101.

Crimmins, E., Saito, Y., & Ingegneri, D. (1989). Changes in life expectancy and disability-free life expectancy in the United States. *Population and Developmental Review, 15,* 235–267.

Cui, X. J., & Vaillant, G. E. (1996). Antecedents and consequences of negative life events in adulthood: A longitudinal study [See comments]. *American Journal of Psychiatry, 153,* 21–26.

Cullen, D. J., Keene, R., Waternaus, C., Knusman, J. M., Caldera, D. L., & Peterson, H. (1984). Results, charges and benefits of intensive care for critically ill patients: Update 1983. *Critical Care Medicine, 12,* 102–106.

Dello Buono, M., Busato, R., Mazzetto, M., Paccagnella, B., Aleotti, F., Zanetti, O., Bianchetti, A., Trabucchi, M., & De Leo, D. (1999). Community care for patients with Alzheimer's disease and non-demented elderly people: Use and satisfaction with services and unmet needs in family caregivers. *International Journal of Geriatric Psychiatry, 14,* 915–924.

DeLongis, A., Cohen, J., Dakof, G., Folkman, S., & Lazarus, R. (1982). Relationship of daily hassles, uplifts, and major life events to health status. *Health Psychology, 1,* 11–136.

Derogatis, L. R. (1977). *The SCL-90 manual I: Scoring, administration and procedures for the SCL-90.* Baltimore: Clinical Psychometric Research.

Diener, E. (1984). Subjective well-being. *Psychological Bulletin, 95,* 542–575.

Dimond, M., Lund, D. A., & Caserta, M. S. (1987). The role of social support in the first two years of bereavement in an elderly sample. *Gerontologist, 27,* 599–604.

Dohrenwend, B. (1983). The epidemiology of mental disorder. In D. Mechanic (Ed.), *Handbook of health, healthcare and the health professions* (pp. 157–194). New York: Free Press.

Duke University. (1978). *Multidimensional functional assessment: The OARS methodology* (2nd ed.). Durham, NC: Duke University.

Emmons, R. (1986). *Personal striving: Toward a theory of personality and subjective well-being.* Unpublished doctoral dissertation, University of Illinois, Urbana-Champaign.

Emmons, R., & Diener, E. (1986). A goal affect analysis of everyday situational choices. *Journal of Research and Personality, 20.*

Ensrud, K. E., et al. (1994). Correlates of impaired function in older women. *Journal of the American Geriatrics Society, 42,* 1155–1160.

Evans, L. K., Yurkow, J., & Siegler, E. L. (1995). The CARE program: A nurse managed collaborative outpatient program to improve function of frail older people. Collaborative assessment and rehabilitation for elders. *Journal of the American Geriatrics Society, 43,* 1155–1160.

Feller, B. (1983, September 14). Americans needing help to function at home. *NCHS Advance Data, 92,* 1–12.

Festinger, L. (1954). A theory of social comparison processes. *Human Relations, 7,* 117–140.

Fiatarone, M. A., Marks, E. C., Ryan, N. D., Meredith, C. N., Lipsitz, L. A., & Evans, W. J. (1990). High-intensity strength training in nonagenarians. Effects on skeletal muscle. *Journal of the American Medical Association, 263,* 3029–3034.

Field, D., & Minkler, M. (1989). Continuity and change in social support between you-old and old-old or very old age. *Journal of Gerontology: Psychological Sciences, 43,* 100–106.

Fillenbaum, G. G. (1988). *Multidimensional functional assessment of older adults.* Hillsdale, NJ: Lawrence Erlbaum.

Finch, J. F., & Zautra, A. J. (1992). Testing latent longitudinal models of social ties and depression among the elderly: A comparison of distribution-free and maximum likelihood estimates with non-normal data. *Psychology and Aging, 7,* 107–118.

Fischer, K., Shaver, P., & Carnochan, P. (1990). How emotions develop and how they organise development. *Cognition and Emotion, 4,* 81–127.

Folkman, S., Lazarus, R., Dunkel-Schetter, C., DeLonges, A., & Gruen, R. (1986). Dynamics of a stressful encounter: Cognitive appraisal, coping, and encounter outcomes. *Journal of Personality and Social Psychology, 50,* 992–1003.

Folkman, S., Lazarus, R., Pimley, S., & Novacek, I. (1987). Age differences in stress and coping processes. *Psychology and Aging, 2,* 171–184.

Ford, A., Haug, M., Jones, P., & Folmar, S. (1990). Race-related differences among elderly urban residents: A cohort study, 1975–1984. *Journals of Gerontology: Social Sciences, 45,* S163–S171

Ford, A., Haug, M., Roy, A., & Folkman, S. (1992). New cohorts of urban elders: Are they in trouble? *Journal of Gerontology: Social Sciences, 47,* S297–S303.

Fowles, D. A. (1998, January 21). A profile of older Americans 1997. *AARP* [On-line]. Available: http://www.aoa.dhhs.gov/aoa/stats/profile

Fowles, D. A. (1998, January 21). A profile of older Americans: 1998 [Statistical profile]. Washington, DC: Administration on Aging. Available: http://www.aoa.dhhs.gov/aoa/stats/profile

Friedman, P. J., Rickmond, D. E., & Basket, J. J. (1988). A prospective trial of serial gait speed as a measure of rehabilitation in the elderly. *Age and Ageing, 17,* 227–235.

Fries, J. F. (1980). Aging, mature death, and the compression of morbidity. *New England Journal of Medicine, 303,* 130–135.

Garfein, A., & Herzog, R. (1995). Robust aging among the young-old, old-old, and oldest-old. *The Journals of Gerontology: Social Sciences, 50B,* S77–S87.

George, L. (1993). Depressive disorders and symptoms in later life. In M. Smyer (Ed.), *Mental health and aging* (pp. 65–74). New York: Springer.

George, L. K. (1989). Stress, social support, and depression over the life course. In K. S. Markides & C. L. Cooper (Eds.), *Aging, stress and health.* New York: Wiley.

George, L. K., & Binstock, R. (Eds.). (1990). *Handbook of aging and the social sciences.* San Diego: Harcourt Brace Jovanovich.

George, L. K., Blazer, D. G., Hughes, D. C., & Fowler, A. M. (1989). Social support and the outcome of major depression. *British Journal of Psychiatry, 154,* 478–485.

Gergen, K. J. (1991). *The saturated self.* New York: Basic Books.

Gibson, R. & Jackson, J. (1992). The black oldest old: Health, functioning, and informal support. In R. Suzman, K. Manton, & D. Willis (Eds.), *The oldest old* (pp. 321–340). New York: Oxford.

Gillick, M. R., Serrell, N. A., & Gillick, L. S. (1982). Adverse consequences of hospitalization in the elderly. *Social Science and Medicine, 16,* 1033–1038.

Goffman, E. (1959). *Presentation of self in everyday life.* Garden City, NY: Doubleday Anchor.

Grasel, E. (1994). Non-pharmacological intervention strategies on aging processes: Empirical data on mental training in "normal" older people and patients with mental impairment. *Archives of Gerontology and Geriatrics, 4*(suppl), 91–98.

Grundy, E. (1997). Progress report—demography and gerontology: Mortality trends among the oldest old. *Ageing and Society, 17,* 713–725.

Guralnik, J. (1991). Prospects for the compression of morbidity. *Journal of Aging and Health, 3,* 138–154.

Guralnik, J., & Kaplan, G. (1989). Predictors of health aging: Prospective evidence from the Alameda County Study. *American Journal of Public Health, 79,* 703–708.

Guralnik, J., LaCroix, A., Everett, D., & Kovar, M. (1989). Aging in the eighties: The prevalence of co-morbidity and its association with disability. *Advance data from vital and health statistics, 170* (DHHS Publication No. PHS 89-1250). Hyattsville, MD: National Center for Health Statistics.

Guralnik, J. M., & Simonsick, E. M. (1993). Physical disability in older Americans. *Journals of Gerontology, 48*(special issue), 3–10.

Gurian, B., & Goisman, R. (1993). Anxiety disorders in the elderly. In M. Smyer (Ed.), *Mental health and aging* (pp. 75–84). New York: Springer.

Gurwitz, A., & Kingsley, T. (1982). *The Cleveland Metropolitan.* Santa Monica, CA: Rand Corporation.

Gurland, B., Cross, P., & Katz, S. (1996). Epidemiological perspectives on opportunities for treatment of depression. *American Journal of Geriatric Psychiatry, 4,* 7–14.

Hall, G. R., Gerdner, L., Zwycart-Stauffacher, M., & Buckwalter, K. C. (1995). Principles of nonpharmacological management: Caring for people with Alzheimer's disease using a conceptual model. *Psychiatric Annals, 25,* 432–440.

Hansson, R. O. (1986). Relational competence, relationships, and adjustments in the old age. *Journal of Personality, 50,* 1050–1058.

Hansson, R. O., Hogan, R., & Jones, W. H. (1984). Affective processes and later life changes: A socioanalytic conceptualization. In C. Izard & C. Malatesta (Eds.), *Emotion in adult development* (pp. 195–209). Beverly Hills, CA: Sage.

Harmon, D. (1991). The aging process: Major risk factors for disease and death. *Proceedings of the National Academy of Sciences USA, 88,* 5360–5363.

Hartmann, D. P. (1977). Considerations in the choice of interobserver reliability estimates. *Journal of Applied Behavior Analysis, 10,* 103–116.

Haug, M. R. (1988). Professional client relationships and the older patient. In S. K. Steinmetz (Ed.), *Family and support systems across the life span* (pp. 225–242). New York: Plenum Press.

Haug, M. R. (1995). Elderly power in the 21st century. *Women and Aging, 7,* 3–10.

Heckhausen, J., & Schultz, R. (1991). *Functional trade-offs in primary and secondary modes of control across the life course: Conceptual issues and overview.* Paper presented at the 11th Biennial Meetings of the International Society for the Study of Behavioral Development, Minneapolis, Minnesota.

Hendricks, J. (1982). Time and social science: History and potential. In E. Mizruchi, B. Glassner, & T. Pastorello (Eds.), *Time and aging: Conceptualization and application in sociological and gerontological research* (pp. 1–45). New York: General Hall, Inc.

Heston, L. L., Garrard, J., Makris, L., Kane, R. L., Cooper, S., Dunham, T., & Zelterman, D. (1992). Inadequate treatment of depressed nursing home elderly. *Journal of the American Geriatrics Society, 40,* 1117–1122.

Hill, R. D., Backman, L., & Fratiglioni, L. (1995). Determinant of functional abilities in dementia. *Journal of the American Geriatrics Society, 43,* 1092–1097.

Hing, E., & Bloom, B. (1990). *Long-term care for the functionally dependent elderly.* Hyattsville, MD: National Center for Health Statistics.

Hirsch, C. H., Sommers, L., Olsen, A., Mullen, J. T., & Winograd, C. (1991). The natural history of functional morbidity in hospitalized older patients. *Journal of the American Geriatrics Society, 38,* 1296–1303.

Hogue, C. C. (1984). Falls and mobility in late life: an ecological model. *Journal of the American Geriatrics Society, 32,* 858–861.

Holahan, C. K. (1988). Relations of life goals at age 70 to activity participation and health and psychological well-being among Terman's gifted men and women. *Psychology and Aging, 3,* 286–291.

Holahan, C. K., & Holahan, C. J. (1987). Self-efficacy, social support and depression in aging: A longitudinal analysis. *Journal of Gerontology, 42,* 65–68.

Holahan, C. K., Holahan, C. J., & Belk, S. (1984). Adjustment in aging: The roles of life stress, hassles and self-efficacy. *Health Psychology, 3,* 315–328.

Holmes, T. H., & Rahe, R. H. (1967). The Social Readjustment Rating Scale. *Journal of Psychosomatic Research, 11,* 213–218.

Hooker, K., & Siegler, I. (1993). Life goals, satisfaction, and self-rated health: Preliminary findings. *Experimental Aging Research, 19,* 97–110.

Horichi, S., & Wilmoth, J. (1998). Deceleration in the age pattern of mortality at older ages. *Demography, 35,* 391–412.

Howland, J., Peterson, E. W., Levin, W. C., Fried, L., Pordon, D., & Bak, S. (1993). Fear of falling among the community dwelling elderly. *Journal of Aging and Health, 5,* 229–243.

Hu, M. H., & Woollacott, M. H. (1994a). Multisensory training of standing balance in older adults: II. Kinematic and electromyographic postural responses. *Journals of Gerontology: Medical Sciences, 49,* M62–M71.

Hu, M. H., & Woollacott, M. H. (1994b). Multisensory training of standing balance in older adults: I. Postural stability and one-leg stance balance. *Journals of Gerontology: Medical Sciences, 49,* M52–M61.

Hu, M. H., & Woollacott, M. (1995). Characteristic patterns of gait in older persons. In B. S. Spivack (Ed.), *Evaluation and management of gait disorders* (pp. 185–197). New York: Marcel Dekker.

Hughes, D. C., Blazer, D. G., & George, L. K. (1988). Age differences in life events: A multivariate controlled analysis. *International Journal of Aging and Human Development, 27,* 207–220.

Hunt, L. A. (1994). Driving and the demented person. In J. C. Morris (Ed.), *Handbook of dementing illnesses* (pp. 529–538). New York: Marcel Dekker, Inc.

Ingersoll-Dayton, B., Morgan, D., & Antonucci, T. (1997). The effects of positive and negative social exchanges on aging adults. *Journal of Gerontology: Social Sciences, 52B,* S190–S199.

Jackson, J. (1988). *The black American elderly.* New York: Springer.

Jacobs, S. (1993). *Pathologic grief.* Washington, DC: American Psychiatric Press.

Jette, A. M., Branch, L. G., & Berlin, J. (1990). Musculoskeletal impairments and physical disablement among the aged. *Journal of Gerontology, 45,* M203–M208.

Johnson, R. J., & Wolinsky, F. D. (1993). The structure of health status among older adults: Disease, disability, functional limitations and perceived health. *Journal of Health and Social Behavior, 34,* 105–121.

Jorm, A. F. (1998). Epidemiology of mental disorders in old age. *Current Opinion in Psychiatry, 11,* 405–409.

Kahana, E., Fairchild, T., & Kahana, B. (1982). Adaptation. In D. J. Mangen & W. A. Peterson (Eds.), *Research instruments in social gerontology: Vol. 1: Clinical and social psychology.* Minneapolis: University of Minnesota.

Kahn, R., & Antonucci, T. C. (1980). Convoy over the life course. In P. B. Baltes & O. A. Brim (Eds.), *Life span development and behavior* (pp. 253–263). New York: Academic Press.

Kanner, A. D., Coyne, J. C., Schaefer, C., & Lazarus, R. (1981). Comparison of two modes of stress measurement: Daily hassles and uplifts vs. major life events. *Journal of Behavioral Medicine, 4,* 1–39.

Kaplan, G. (1992). Maintenance of functioning in the elderly. *Annals of Epidemiology, 2,* 823–834.

Kaplan, G., Barell, V., & Lusky, A. (1988). Subjective state of health and survival in elderly adults. *Journal of Gerontology: Social Sciences, 43,* 114–120.

Kaplan, G., Strawbridge, W., Camacho, T., & Cohen, R. (1993). Factors associated with change in physical functioning in the elderly: A six-year prospective study. *Journal of Aging and Health, 5,* 140–154.

Kastenbaum, R. (1963). Cognitive and personal futurity in later life. *Journal of Individual Psychology, 19,* 216–222.

Kastenbaum, R. (1982). Time course and time perspective in later life. *Annual Review of Gerontology and Geriatrics, 3,* 80–101.

Kathol, R. G., & Petty, F. (1981). Relationship of depression to medical illness: A critical review. *Journal of Affective Disorders, 3,* 112

Katz, S., & Akpom, C. A. (1976). 12. Index of ADL. *Medical Care, 14*(suppl), 116–118.

Katz, S., Branch, L., Brown, M., Papsidero, J., Beck, J., & Greer, D. (1983). Active life expectancy. *New England Journal of Medicine, 309,* 1218–1224.

Katz, S., Ford, A., Moskowitz, R., Jackson, B., & Jaffe, M. (1963). Studies of illness in aged, index of ADL: Standardized measure of biological and psychosocial function. *Journal of the American Medical Association, 165,* 84–94.

Katz, S., Ford, A., Moskowitz, R., Jackson, D., & Jaffee, M. W. (1963). Studies of illness in the aged: The index of ADL. *Journal of American Medical Association, 185,* 94.

Kaufman, T. (1983). Relationship of hip extension strength and standup ability in geriatric patients. *Physical and Occupational Therapy in Geriatrics, 1,* 39–41.

Kendler, K. S., Kessler, R. C., Heath, A. C., & Eaves, L. J. (1993). A twin study of recent life events and difficulties. *Archives of General Psychiatry, 50,* 789–796.

Kessler, R. C. (1983). Psychosocial stress. In H. Kaplan (Ed.), *Methodological issues in the study of psychosocial stress.* San Diego: Academic Press.

Kessler, R. C. (1997). The effects of stressful life events on depression. *Annual Review of Psychology, 48,* 191–214.

Kessler, R. C., Kendler, K. S., Heath, A., Neale, M. C., & Eaves, L. J. (1992). Social support, depressed mood, and adjustment to stress: A genetic epidemiologic investigation. *Journal of Personality and Social Psychology, 62,* 257–272.

Kessler, R. C., & Magee, W. J. (1994). The disaggregation of vulnerability to depression as a function of the determinants of onset and recurrence. In W. R. Avison & I. H. Gotlib (Eds.), *Stress and mental health: Contemporary issues and prospects for the future* (pp. 239–258). New York: Plenum.

Kim, J. S., Bramlett, M. H., Wright, L. K., & Poon, L. W. (1998). Racial differences in health status and health behaviors of older adults. *Nursing Research, 47,* 243–250.

Kirk, R. (1982). *Experimental design: Procedures for the behavioral sciences.* Belmont, CA: Brooks/Cole.

Koroknay, V. J., Werner, P., Cohen-Mansfield, J., & Braun, J. (1995). Maintaining ambulation in the frail nursing home resident: A nursing administered walking program. *Journal of Gerontological Nursing, 21,* 18–24.

Kovar, M. (1988). Aging in the eighties: People living alone—two years later. *Advance Data, 146,* April 4.

Koyano, W., Shibata, H., Haga, H., & Suyama, Y. (1986). Prevalence and outcome of low ADL and incontinence among the elderly: Five-year follow-up in a Japanese urban community. *Archives of Gerontology and Geriatrics, 5,* 197–206.

Krause, N. (1986). Stress and coping: Reconceptualizing the role of locus of control beliefs. *Journal of Gerontology, 41,* 617–622.

Krause, N. (1987a). Chronic financial strain, social support, and depressive symptoms among older adults. *Psychology and Aging, 2,* 185–192.

Krause, N. (1987b). Chronic strain, locus of control and distress in older adults. *Psychology and Aging, 2,* 375–382.

Krause, N. (1987c). Life stress, social support, and self-esteem in an elderly population. *Psychology and Aging, 2,* 340–356.

Krause, N., & Jay, G. (1991). Stress, social support and negative interaction in later life. *Research on Aging, 13,* 333–363.

Krause, N., & Markides, K. (1990). Measuring social support among older adults. *International Journal of Aging and Human Development, 30,* 37–53.

Krippendorff, K. (1980). *Content analysis: An introduction to its methodology.* Beverly Hills: Sage.

Krishnan, K. R., George, L. K., Pieper, C. F., Jiang, W., Arias, R., Look, A., & O'Connor, C. (1998). Depression and social support in elderly patients with cardiac disease. *American Heart Journal, 136,* 491–495.

Kuetner. (1992) ???. In M. Ory (Ed.), *Aging, health and behavior.* Newbury Park, CA: Sage.

Labouvie-Vief, G., Chiodo, L., Goguen, L. A., & Diehl, M. (1995). Representation of self across the life span. *Psychology and Aging, 10,* 404–415.

Landefeld, C. S., Palmer, R., Kowal, J., Kresevic, D. M., & Rosenblatt, M. (1990). Functional decline in acutely ill old patients: Incidence, course and risk factors. *Clinical Research, 39,* 580A.

Langer, E. J., & Rodin, J. (1976). The effects of choice and enhanced personal responsibility for the aged: A field experiment in an institutional setting. *Journal of Personality and Social Psychology, 34,* 191–198.

Lapierre, S., Bouffard, L., & Bastin, E. (1992–1993). Motivational goal objects in later life. *International Aging and Human Development, 36,* 279–292.

Larkin, M. (1999, March 27). Centenarians point the way to healthy aging. *Lancet, 353,* 1074.

Lawrence, R. H., & Jette, A. M. (1996). Disentangling the disablement process. *Journals of Gerontology: Social Sciences, 51,* S173–S182.

Lawton, M. P. (1982). Competence, environmental press, and the adaptation of older people. In M. P. Lawton, P. G. Windley, & T. O. Byerts (Eds.), *Aging and the environment: Theoretical approaches* (pp. 33–59). New York: Springer.

Lawton, M. P., & Nahemow, L. (1973). Ecology and the aging process. In C. Eisdorfer & M. P. Lawton (Eds.), *The psychology of adult development and aging* (pp. 619–674). Washington, DC: American Psychological Association.

Lazarus, R., & DeLongis, A. (1983). Psychological stress and coping in aging. *American Psychologist, 40,* 770–779.

Lazarus, R., DeLongis, A., Folkman, S., & Gruen, R. (1985). Stress and adaptational outcomes. The problem of confounded measures. *American Psychology, 40,* 770–785.

Lazarus, R., & Folkman, S. (1984). *Stress, appraisal and coping.* New York: Springer.

Lazarus, R., & Launier, R. (1978). Perspectives in interaction psychology. In L. A. Pearlin & M. Lewis (Eds.), *Stress-related transactions between person and environment.* New York: Plenum.

Lazarus, R. A., & Launier, R. (1978). Stress-related transactions between person and environment. In L. A. Perlin & M. Lewis (Eds.), *Perspectives in interaction psychology.* New York: Plenum.

Lebowitz, B. (1996). Diagnosis and treatment of depression in late life: An overview of the NIH Consensus Statement. *American Journal of Geriatric Psychiatry, 4*(suppl).

Lewis, C. N. (1971). Reminiscing and self-concept in old age. *Journal of Gerontology, 26,* 240–243.

Linzer, M., Spitzer, R. K., Kroenke, K., Williams, J. B., Hahn, S., Brody, D., & deGruy, F. (1996). Gender, quality of life, and mental disorders in primary care: Results for the PRIME-MD 1000 study. *American Journal of Medicine, 101,* 526–533.

MacFadyen, D. (1990). International demographic trends. In R. L. Kane, J. Grimley Evans, & D. MacFadyen (Eds.), *Improving the health of older people: A world view* (pp. 19–29). Oxford: World Health Organization.

Maddox, G., & Douglas, E. (1973). Self assessment of health: A longitudinal study of elderly subjects. *Journal of Health and Social Behavior, 14,* 87–93.

Manton, K. (1988). A longitudinal study of functional change and mortality in the United States. *Journal of Gerontology, 43,* 153–161.

Manton, K., Stallard, E., & Tolley, H. (1991). Limits to human life expectancy: Evidence, prospects, and implications. *Population and Developmental Review, 17,* 603–637.

Marcus, H., & Herzog, A. R. (1991). The role of the self-concept in aging. *Annual Review of Gerontology and Geriatrics, 12.*

Martin, P., Poon, L. W., Kim, E., & Johnson, M. A. (1996). Social and psychological resources in the oldest old. *Experimental Aging and Research, 22,* 121–139.

Maurer, B. T., Stern, A. G., Kinossian, B., Cook, K. D., & Schumacher, H. R. (1999). Osteoarthritis of the knee: Isokinetic quadriceps exercise versus an educational intervention. *Archives of Physical Medicine and Rehabilitation, 80,* 1293–1299.

Mayring, P. (1987). Subjektives wohlbefinden im alter: Stand der forschung und theoretische weiterentwicklung. *Zeitschrift fur Gerontologie, 20,* 367–376.

McKitrick, L. A., Camp, C. J., & Black, F. W. (1995). Prospective memory intervention in Alzheimer's disease. *Journals of Gerontology: Psychological Sciences, 47,* P337–P343.

McMurdo, M. E., & Rennie, L. (1993). A controlled trial of exercise by residents of old people's homes. *Age and Ageing, 22,* 11–15.

McVey, L. J., Becker, P. M., & Saltz, C. C. (1989). Effect of a geriatric consultation team on functional status of elderly hospitalized patients. *Annals of Internal Medicine, 110,* 79–84.

Mendes de Leon, C. F., Seeman, T. E., Baker, D. I., Richardson, E. D., & Tinetti, M. E. (1996). Self-efficacy, physical decline, and change in functioning in community-living elders: A prospective study. *Journals of Gerontology: Social Sciences, 51B,* S183–S190.

Mermelstein, R., Miller, B., Prohaska, T., Benson, V., & Van Nostrand, J. (1993). Measures of health. In U.S. Dept. of Health and Human Services, *Vital and health statistics* (Vol. 3, pp. 9–13). Washington, DC: U.S. Government Printing Office.

Mirowsky, J. (1995). Age and sense of control. *Social Psychology Quarterly, 58,* 31–43.

Mossey, J., & Shapiro, E. (1982). Self rated health: A predictor of mortality among the elderly. *American Journal of Public Health, 8,* 800–808.

Moxley Scarborough, D., Krebs, D. E., & Harris, B. A. (1998). Quadriceps muscle strength and dynamic stability in elderly persons. *Age and Ageing, 27*(suppl), 12–16.

Musil, C. (1998). Health stress, coping and social support in grandmother caregivers. *Health Care for Women International, 19,* 441–455.

Nagi, S. Z. (1991). Disability concepts revisited. In A. M. Pope & A. R. Tarlov (Eds.), *Disability in America: Toward a national agenda for prevention* (pp. 309–327). Washington, DC: National Academy Press.

National Center for Health Statistics. (1984). Birth, marriages, divorces, and deaths for 1983. NCHS monthly vital statistics report (provisional data from the National Center for Health Statistics, Vol. 32, No. 12). (DHHS Publication No. PHS 84-1120). Washington, DC: U.S. Government Printing Office.

Nuttin, J. (1984). *Motivation, planning and action: A relational theory of behavioral dynamics.* Hillsdale, NJ: Erlbaum.

Olshensky, S., & Carnes, B. (1994). Demographic perspectives on human senescence. *Population and Developmental Review, 20,* 57–80.

Olshensky, S., Carnes, B., & Cassel, C. (1990). In search of Methuselah: Estimating the upper limits of human longevity. *Science, 250,* 634–640.

Olshensky, S., Rudberg, M., Cassel, C., & Brody, J. (1991). Trading off longer life for worsening health. *Journal of Aging and Health, 3,* 194–216.

Olshensky, S. J., & Wilkins, R. (1998). Introduction—Policy implications of the measure and trends in health expectancy. *Journal of Aging and Health, 10,* 123–135.

O'Reilly, S. C., Muir, K. R., & Doherty, M. (1999). Effectiveness of home exercise on pain and disability from osteoarthritis of the knee: A randomized controlled trial. *Annals of Rheumatic Disease, 58,* 15–19.

Ormel, J., Kempen, G. I., Penninx, B. W., Brilman, E. I., Beekman, A. T., & van Sonderen, E. (1997). Chronic medical conditions and mental health in older people: Disability and psychosocial resources mediate specific mental health effects. *Psychology and Medicine, 27,* 1065–1077.

Ostwald, S., Snowdon, D., Rysavy, D., Keenam, N., & Kane, R. (1989). Manual dexterity as a correlate of dependency in the elderly. *Journal of the American Geriatrics Society, 37,* 963–969.

Oxman, T. C., Berkman, L. F., Kasl, S., Freeman, D. H., & Barret, J. (1992). Social support and depressive symptoms in the elderly. *Journal of Epidemiology, 135,* 356–368.

Parker, M., Thorslund, M., & Nordstrom, M. (1992). Predictors of mortality for the oldest old: A 4-year follow-up of community based elderly in Sweden. *Archives of Gerontology and Geriatrics, 14,* 227–237.

Pearlin, L. I., Menaghan, E., Lieberman, M. A., & Mullen, J. T. (1981). The stress process. *Journal of Health and Social Behavior, 22,* 337–356.

Pearlin, L. I., & Schooler, C. (1978). The structure of coping. *Journal of Health and Social Behavior, 19,* 2–21.

Penninx, B. W., Guralnik, J. M., Simonsick, E. M., Kasper, J. D., Ferrucci, L., & Fried, L. P. (1998). Emotional vitality among disabled older women: The Women's Health and Aging Study [see comments]. *Journal of the American Geriatrics Society, 46,* 807–815.

Penninx, B. W., van Tilburg, T., Deeg, D. J., Kriegsman, D. M., Boeke, A. J., & van Eijk, J. T. (1997). Direct and buffer effects of social support and personal coping resources in individuals with arthritis. *Social Science and Medicine, 44,* 393–402.

Perls, T., & Silver, M. (1999). *Living to 100—Lessons in living your maximum potential at any age.* New York: Basic Books.

Perls, T., & Wood, E. (1996). Acute care costs of the oldest old. *Archives of Internal Medicine, 156,* 754–760.

Pescatello, L. S., & Judge, J. O. (1995). The impact of physical activity and physical fitness on functional capacity in older adults. In B. S. Spivack (Ed.), *Evaluation and management of gait disorders* (pp. 325–339). New York: Marcel Dekker.

Pitskhelauri, G. Z. (1983). *The long living of Soviet Georgia.* New York: Human Sciences Press.

Poon, L. W., Clayton, G. M., Martin, P., Johnson, M. A., Courtenay, B. C., Sweaney, A. L., Merriam, S. B., & Pless, B. S. (1992). The Georgia Centenarian Study. *International Journal of Aging and Human Development, 34,* 1–17.

Poon, L. W., Martin, P., Clayton, G. M., Messner, S., Noble, C. A., & Johnson, M. A. (1992). The influences of cognitive resources on adaptation and old age [see comments]. *International Journal of Aging and Human Development, 34,* 31–46.

Pruchno, R. A., Burant, C. J., & Peters, N. D. (1997). Coping strategies of people living in multigenerational households: effects on well-being. *Psychology and Aging, 12,* 115–124.

Pyszczynski, T., & Greenberg, J. (1992). *Hanging on and letting go: Understanding the onset, progression, and remission of depression.* New York: Springer

Quayhagen, M. P., & Quayhagen, M. (1989). Differential effects of family-based strategies on Alzheimer's disease. *Gerontologist, 29,* 150–155.

Rakowski, W. (1979). Future time perspective in later adulthood: Review and research directions. *Experimental Aging Research, 5,* 43–88.

Ranga, R. K., George, L. K., Peiper, C. F., et al. (1998). Depression and social support in elderly patients with cardiac disease. *American Heart Journal, 136,* 491–495.

Rantanen, T., Guralnik, J. M., Ferrucci, L., Leveille, S., & Fried, L. P. (1999). Coimpairments: Strength and balance as predictors of severe walking disability. *Journals of Gerontology: Medical Sciences, 54,* M172–M176.

Rantanen, T., Guralnik, J. M., Sakari-Rantala, R., Leveille, S., Simonsick, E. M., Ling, S., & Fried, L. P. (1999). Disability, physical activity, and muscle strength in older women: The Women's Health and Aging Study. *Archives of Physical and Medical Rehabilitation, 90,* 130–135.

Rapkin, B., & Fischer, K. (1992). Personal goals of older adults: Issues in assessment and prediction. *Psychology and Aging, 7,* 127–137.

Revicki, D., & Mitchell, J. (1990). Strain, social support, and mental health in rural elderly individuals. *Journal of Gerontology: Social Sciences, 45,* S267–S274.

Rice, D., & LaPlante, M. (1988). Chronic illness, disability, and increasing longevity. In S. Sullivan & M. E. Lewis (Eds.), *Ethics and economics of long-term care.* Washington, DC: American Enterprise Institute.

Richardson, V. (1992). Service use among urban African American elderly people. *Social Work, 37,* 47–54.

Riggs, J., & Millecchia, D. (1992). Mortality among the elderly in the U. S., 1956–1987: Demonstration of the upper boundary to Gompertzian mortality. *Mechanisms of Aging and Development, 62,* 191–199.

Roberts, B. L. (1989). Effects of walking on balance among elders. *Nursing Research, 38,* 180–182.

Roberts, B. L. (1999). Activities of daily living: Factors related to independence. In A. S. Hinshaw, S. L. Feetham, & J. L. F. Shaver (Eds.), *Handbook of clinical nursing research* (pp. 563–578). London: Sage.

Roberts, B. L., & Algase, D. L. (1988). Alzheimer's victims and the environment. *Nursing Clinics of North America, 23,* 83–93.

Roberts, B. L., Anthony, M. K., Matejczyk, M., & Moore, D. (1994). The relationship of social support to functional limitations, pain and well-being among men and women. *Journal of Women and Aging, 6,* 3–19.

Roberts, B. L., Dunkle, R., & Haug, M. (1994). Physical, psychological, and social resources as moderators of the relationship of stress to mental health of the very old. *Journal of Gerontology: Social Sciences, 49,* S35–S43.

Roberts, B. L., Matecjyck, M. B., & Anthony, M. (1996). The effects of social support on the relationship of functional limitations and pain to depression. *Arthritis Care and Research, 9,* 67–73.

Roberts, B. L., Srour, M. I., Mansour, J. M., Palmer, R. M., & Wagner, M. B. (1994). The effects of a 12-week aerobic walking program on postural stability of healthy elderly. In K. Taguchi, M. Igarashi, & S. Mori (Eds.), *Vestibular and neural front* (pp. 215–218). New York: Elsevier.

Roberts, B. L., Wagner, M., Palmer, R., Mansour, J. M., & Srour, M. I. (1993). Muscle strength and endurance among healthy elderly adults [abstract]. *Physical Therapy, 73,* S37.

Roberts, B. L., & Wykle, M. L. (1993). Pilot study results. Falls among institutionalized elderly. *Journal of Gerontological Nursing, 19,* 13–20.

Roberts, R. E., Kaplan, G. A., Sherma, S. J., & Strawbridge, W. J. (1997). Does growing old increase the risk of depression? *American Journal of Psychiatry, 154,* 1384–1390.

Robichaud, L., Hébert, R., Roy, P., & Roy, C. (2000). A preventive program for community-dwelling elderly at risk of functional decline: A pilot study. *Archives of Gerontology and Geriatrics, 30,* 73–84.

Robins, L. N., & Reiger, D. A. (1991). *Psychiatric disorders in America: The epidemiologic catchment area study.* New York: Free Press.

Rodgers, W., & Miller, B. (1997). A comparative analysis of ADL questions in surveys of older people. *Journal of Gerontology, 52B* (special issue), 21–36.

Rodin, J. (1986). Health, control and aging. In M. M. Baltes & P. B. Baltes (Eds.), *The psychology of aging and control* (pp. 139–165). Hillsdale, NJ: Erlbaum.

Rodin, J. (1989, May). Sense of control: Potentials for intervention. *Annals of the New York Academy of Psychological and Social Sciences, 503,* 29–42.

Rodin & Timko. (1992).

Rogers, A., & Belanger, A. (1989). Active life among the elderly in the United States: Multi state life-table estimates and population projections. *Milbank Quarterly/Health and Society, 67,* 370–411.

Rook, K. S. (1994). Assessing the health-related dimensions of older adults' social relationships. In M. P. Lawton & J. A. Teresi (Eds.), *Annual review of gerontology and geriatrics.* New York: Springer.

Roos, N., & Havens, B. (1991). Predictors of successful aging: A twelve year study of Manitoba elderly. *American Journal of Public Health, 81*, 63–68.

Rosenberg, M. (1965). *Society and self-image.* Princeton: Princeton University Press.

Rosenberg, M. (1979). *Conceiving the self.* New York: Basic Books.

Rosencranz, H. A., & Philblad, C. T. (1970). Measuring the health of the elderly. *Journal of Gerontology, 25*, 129–133.

Rosenwaike, I. (1985). *The extreme aged in America.* Westport, CT: Greenwood Press.

Rosow, I. (1985). Status and role change through the life cycle. In R. H. Binstock & E. Shanas (Eds.), *Handbook of aging and the social sciences* (pp. 62–93). New York: Van Nostrand Reinhold.

Ross, C., & Van Willigen, M. (1997). Education and the subjective quality of life. *Journal of Health and Social Behavior, 38*, 275–297.

Rosswurm, M. A. (1989). Assessment of perceptual processing deficits in persons with Alzheimer's disease. *Western Journal of Nursing Research, 11*, 458–468.

Rowe, J. W., & Kahn, R. L. (1998). *Successful aging.* New York: Pantheon Books.

Russell, D. W., & Cutrona, C. E. (1991). Social support, stress, and depressive symptoms among the elderly: Test of a process model. *Psychology and Aging, 6*, 201

Sanborn, B., & Bould, S. (1989). Formal services. In S. Bould, B. Sanborn, & L. Reif (Eds.), *Eighty-five plus: The oldest old* (pp. 147–172). Belmont, CA: Wadsworth Publishing.

Sarason, I. G., Sarason, B. R., Potter, E. H., & Antoni, M. H. (1985). Life events, social support, and illness. *Psychosomatic Medicine, 47*, 156–163.

Schilke, J. M., Johnson, G. O., Housh, T. J., & O'Dell, J. R. (1996). Effects of muscle-strength training on the functional status of patients with osteoarthritis of the knee joint. *Nursing Research, 45*, 68–72.

Schneider, L. S. (1995). Efficacy of clinical treatment for mental disorders among older persons. In M. Gatz (Ed.), *Emerging issues in mental health and aging* (pp. 19–72). Washington, DC: American Psychological Association.

Schoenfeld, D., Malmrose, L., Blazer, D., Gold, D., & Seeman, T. (1994). Self-rated health and mortality in the high functioning elderly—a close look at healthy individuals: MacArthur field study of successful aging. *The Journals of Gerontology: Medical Sciences, 49*, M109–M115.

Schrauger, J. S., & Schoeneman, T. J. (1979). Symbolic interactional view of self-concept: Through the looking-glass darkly. *Psychological Bulletin, 86*, 549–573.

Schulz, R., Heckhausen, J., & Locher, J. L. (1991). Adult development, control, and adaptive functioning. *Journal of Social Issues, 47,* 177–196.

Scogin, F., & McElreath, L. (1994). Efficacy of psychosocial treatments for geriatric depression: A quantitative review. *Journal of Consulting and Clinical Psychology, 62,* 69–74.

Seeman, T., Charpentier, P., Berkman, L., Tinetti, M., Guralnik, J., Albert, M., Blazer, D., & Rowe, J. (1994). Predicting changes in physical performance in a high functioning elderly cohort: MacArthur studies of successful aging. *Journals of Gerontology: Medical Sciences, 49,* M97–M108.

Seeman, T. E., Unger, J. B., McAvay, G., & Mendes de Leon, C. F. (1999). Self-efficacy beliefs and perceived declines in functional ability: MacArthur studies of successful aging. *Journals of Gerontology: Psychological Sciences, 54B,* P214–P222.

Selye, H. (1956). *The stress of life.* New York: McGraw-Hill.

Shorter, E. (1992). *From paralysis to fatigue.* New York: Free Press.

Siegel, J., & Taeuber, C. (1993). Demographic perspectives on the long lived society. *Daedalus, 115,* 77–118.

Silber, E., & Tippett, J. (1965). Self-esteem: Clinical assessment in measurement validation. *Psychological Reports, 16,* 1017–1071.

Simons, R. L., & West, G. E. (1985). Life changes, coping resources, and health among the elderly. *International Journal of Aging and Human Development, 20,* 173–189.

Smith, D. (1997). Centenarians: Human longevity outliers. *The Gerontologist, 37,* 200–207.

Smith, R., & Baltes, R. B. (1999). Trends and profiles of psychological functioning in very old age. In P. B. Baltes & K. U. Mayer (Eds.), *The Berlin aging study: Aging from 70–100.* New York: Cambridge University Press.

Sobell, L. G., Toneatto, T., Sobell, M. B., Schuller, R., & Maxwell, M. (1990). A procedure for reducing error in reports of life events. *Journal of Psychosomatic Research, 2,* 163–170.

Soldo, B. J., & Myllyluoma, J. (1983). Caregivers who live with dependent elderly. *Gerontologist, 23,* 605–611.

Sterns, H., Barrett, G., & Alexander, R. (1985). Accidents and the aging individual. In J. Birren & K. W. Schaie (Eds.), *Handbook of the psychology of aging* (2nd ed., pp. 703–724). New York: Van Nostrand Reinhold Co.

Stewart, A. L., & King, A. C. (1991). Evaluating the efficacy of physical activity for influencing quality of life outcomes in older adults. *Annals of Behavioral Medicine, 13,* 108–116.

Strawbridge, W., Kaplan, G., Camacho, T., & Cohen, R. (1992). The dynamics of disability and functional change in an elderly cohort: Results from the Alameda County Study. *Journal of the American Geriatric Society, 40,* 799–806.

Sugarman, S. (1987). *Piaget's construction of the child's reality.* Cambridge: Cambridge University Press.

Suls, J., & Miller, R. (1977). *Social comparison processes: Theoretical and empirical perspectives.* New York: John Wiley and Sons.

Suls, J., & Mullen, B. (1982). From the cradle to the grave: Comparison and self evaluation across the lifespan. In J. Suls (Ed.), *Psychological perspectives on the self* (pp. 97–128). Hillsdale, NJ: Lawrence Erlbaum.

Suzman, R., Manton, K., & Willis, D. (1992). Introducing the oldest old. In R. Suzman, K. Manton, & D. Willis (Eds.), *The oldest old* (pp. 3–14). New York: Oxford.

Taeuber, C., & Rosenwaike, I. (1992). A demographic portrait of America's oldest old. In R. Suzman, K. Manton, & D. Willis (Eds.), *The oldest old* (pp. 17–49). New York: Oxford.

Tennstedt, S., Sullivan, L., McKinlay, J., & D'Agostino, R. (1990). How important is function status as a predictor of service use by older people? *Journal of Aging and Health, 2,* 439–461.

Theorell, T., & Emlund, N. (1993). On physiological effects of positive and negative life changes—a longitudinal study. *Journal of Psychosomatic Research, 37,* 653–659.

Thoits, P. A. (1983). Multiple identities and psychological well-being: A reformulation and test of the social isolation hypothesis. *American Sociological Review, 48,* 174–187.

Thorlund, M., Norstrom, T., & Wernberg, K. (1991). The utilization of home help in Sweden: A multivariate analysis. *The Gerontologist, 31,* 116–119.

Tideiksaar, R. (1998). *Falls in older persons: Prevention and management.* New York: Marcel Dekker.

Tinetti, M. E., Mendes de Leon, C. F., Doucette, J. T., & Baker, D. I. (1994). Fear of falling and fall-related efficacy in relationship to functioning among community-living elders. *Journal of Gerontology, 49,* M140–M147.

Topp, R., Mikesky, A., Wigglesworth, J., Holt, W. J., & Edwards, J. E. (1993). The effect of a 12-week dynamic resistance strength training program on gait velocity and balance of older adults. *Gerontologist, 33,* 501–506.

Tse, S. K., & Bailey, D. M. (1992). Tai chi and postural control in the well elderly. *American Journal of Occupational Therapy, 46,* 295–300.

Turner, R. J., & Noh, S. (1988). Physical disability and depression: A longitudinal analysis. *Journal of Health and Social Behavior, 29,* 23–37.

United Nations. (1991). *United Nations demographic yearbook.* New York: United Nations.

Unutzer, J., Patrick, D. L., & Simon, G. (1997). Depressive symptoms and the cost of health services in HMO patients aged 65 years and older. *Journal of the American Medical Association, 277,* 1618–1623.

U.S. Department of Health and Human Services. (1989). *The national nursing home survey; 1985 summary for the United States.* Washington, DC: U.S. Government Printing Office.

U.S. General Accounting Office. (1998). *Alzheimer's disease: Estimates of prevalence in the United States.* Washington, DC: U.S. Government Printing Office.

Vampel, J. (1998). Demographic analysis of aging and longevity. *The American Economic Review, 88,* 242–247.

Van Nostrand, J., Furner, S. E., & Suzman, R. (1993). Introduction. In U.S. Department of Health and Human Services (Ed.), *Vital and health statistics* (pp. 1–4). Washington, DC: U.S. Government Printing Office.

van Tilburg, T. (1998). Losing and gaining in old age: Changes in personal network size and social support in a four-year longitudinal study. *Journal of Gerontology: Social Sciences, 53,* S313–S323.

Verbrugge, L. (1990). Disability. *Rheumatic Disease Clinics of North America, 16,* 741–761.

Vita, A., Terry, R., Hebert, H., & Fries, I. (1998). Aging health risks and cumulative disability. *New England Journal of Medicine, 338,* 1035–1041.

Wallston, K. A., Brown, G. K., Stein, M. J., & Dobbins, C. J. (1989). Comparing the short and long versions of the arthritis impact measurement scales. *Journal of Rheumatology, 16,* 1105–1109.

Weil, A. (1995). *Spontaneous healing.* New York: Fawcett and Columbine.

Weinberger, M., Hiner, S., & Tierney, W. (1985). In support of hassles as a measure of stress in predicting health outcomes. *Journal of Behavioral Medicine, 10,* 19–31.

Weiner, P., Alexopoulos, G. S., Kakuma, T., Meyers, B. S., Rosenthal, E., & Chester, J. (1997). The limits of history taking in geriatric depression. *American Journal of Geriatric Psychiatry, 5,* 116–125.

Wheaton, B. (1984). Models for the stress-buffering functions of coping responses. *Journal of Health and Social Behavior, 26,* 352–364.

Zarit, S., Johansson, B., & Berg, S. (1993, August). Functional impairment and co-disability in the oldest-old. *Journal of Aging and Health, 5,* 291–305.

Zarit, S., Johansson, B., & Malmberg, B. (1995). Changes in functional competency in the oldest old. *Journal of Aging and Health, 7,* 3–23.

Zautra, A. J., & Reich, J. W. (1983). Life events and perceptions of life quality: Developments in a two-factor approach. *Journal of Community Psychology, 1,* 121–132.

Index